People Before the Park

▶ ▶ ▶ ▶ ▶ ▶ ▶ ◈ ◀ ◀ ◀ ◀ ◀ ◀ ◀

People Before the Park

The Kootenai and Blackfeet Before Glacier National Park

SALLY THOMPSON

KOOTENAI CULTURE COMMITTEE

PIKUNNI TRADITIONAL ASSOCIATION

Montana Historical Society Press

Helena, Montana

Front cover photograph: Running Eagle Falls, T. J. Hileman, photographer,
Schultz Collection, Merrill G. Burlingame Special Collections,
Montana State University Libraries, Bozeman, 248 (color added)
Frontispiece photograph: Two Medicine Lake,
T. J. Hileman, photographer, Glacier National Park, 1107

Cover and book design by Diane Gleba Hall
Typeset in Adobe Caslon
Printed in the United States

Distributed by National Book Network, 4501 Forbes Boulevard, Suite 200,
Lanham, MD 20706, (800) 462-6420, http://www.nbnbooks.com/

16 17 18 19 20 21 22 23 24   10 9 8 7 6 5 4 3 2

This project is funded in part by a grant from Humanities Montana,
an affiliate of the National Endowment for the Humanities. The findings
and conclusions in this publication are the views of the authors and do not
necessarily represent the views of Humanities Montana or the
National Endowment for the Humanities.

Humanities **MONTANA**

All proceeds to benefit the Montana Historical Society.

Library of Congress Cataloging-in-Publication Data
Thompson, Sally (Sally N.)
People before the park : the Kootenai and Blackfeet before
Glacier National Park / Sally Thompson ; Kootenai Culture Committee ;
Pikunni Traditional Association.

pgs. cm

Includes bibliographical references and index.
ISBN 978-1-940527-71-0 (paperback : alkaline paper)
ISBN 978-1-940527-82-6 (hardcover : alkaline paper)
1. Kootenai Indians—Montana—History. 2. Siksika Indians—
Montana—History. 3. Glacier National Park Region (Mont.)—History.
4. Kootenai Indians—Montana—Social life and customs. 5. Siksika
Indians—Montana—Social life and customs. 6. Mountain life—Montana—
History. 7. Montana—Social life and customs. 8. Names, Geographical—
Montana—Glacier National Park. 9. 9781940527710 I. Kootenai Culture
Committee. II. Pikunni Traditional Association. III. Title.

E99.K85T47 2014
978.6'01—dc23
2014023755

*The Montana Historical Society
gratefully acknowledges the financial support
provided for this publication by*

❖

BNSF Railway Association

Charles Redd Center for Western Studies

Dr. Laurie M. Arnold

Humanities Montana

Pendleton and Elisabeth Carey Miller
Charitable Foundation

Contents

◈

Preface

◈

In September 2008, I was contracted by Glacier National Park to write
a book about tribes of the area and their use of the lands now within the
park. Chief of natural and cultural resources Jack Potter initiated the
project so that park visitors would know that the area was not devoid of
people prior to the park's creation in 1910. This effort was also intended to
replace the stereotypical images of the Native peoples of the region that
had been promoted by the Great Northern Railway in the early years of
the park.

After park officials had initiated contact with the Blackfeet Nation
and the Confederated Salish and Kootenai Tribes about the project, I met
with appointed representatives of the tribes to discuss the project and to
invite their participation. With the steady and sage advice of the park's
cultural resource specialist, Lon Johnson, and the able archival assistance
of Deirdre Shaw, we set about to create a collaborative process that would
lead toward a successful book. We first imagined a book that would provide a complete overview of park use, from the earliest archaeological
evidence right up through the political decisions that led to the creation
of the park. My job would be to review all that had been researched and
written before me, with an emphasis on the traditional camp areas, the
food-gathering areas, and the trails that connected one place to another.
Working with the tribes, we would together compile oral histories to
bring these places and associated activities to life.

Given certain political issues, historical issues of trust between tribes
and anthropologists, and controversial interpretations of spotty archaeological data, it soon became clear that our initial goal wasn't going to

be easy to reach. A new approach was needed. Many meetings and six months later, we had a new structure in place. The Kootenai Culture Committee agreed to participate, noting an opportunity to correct common misperceptions, and committee members assigned the oversight of the project to Vernon Finley and Naida Lefthand. The Blackfeet Tribal Council, led by Chairman Willie Sharp, accepted a plan for the Pikunni Traditional Association to oversee the Blackfeet effort, which would be coordinated by Smokey and Darnell Rides At The Door.

We mutually agreed to narrow the focus of the book to the seasonal rounds of these two tribes, the Kootenai and the Blackfeet, during the nineteenth century. The more limited temporal focus precluded the need to delve into the vagueness of precontact archaeology and avoided unresolved political issues between the Blackfeet and Glacier Park. It allowed us to focus on the richness of the tribes' lifeways and the vast knowledge required to live in and around these mountains.

This project provided a rare opportunity for me, an anthropologist, to collaborate with tribal representatives as they recalled these old lifeways. Two key events, one involving each tribe, initiated the project. The goal of these gatherings was to engage as many elders and advisors as possible in this process.

Kootenai and Ktunaxa elders from five of the seven bands gathered at the University of Montana Biological Research Station at Yellow Bay on Flathead Lake in April 2009 for a two-day event cosponsored by the University of Montana–Missoula's Experimental Program to Stimulate Competitive Research for the National Science Foundation (NSF-EP-SCoR). We focused on memories of the Glacier area. The Tobacco Plains Ktunaxa, in particular, had managed to maintain a close relationship with the park area well into the twentieth century because of their particular history and geographic proximity. They had much to contribute, as did the Ksanka Band based in Elmo.

For the Blackfeet, Smokey and Darnell Rides At The Door organized a day-long gathering in July 2009 in their painted lodge, inviting bundle holders and other knowledgeable elders from the four directions of the Blackfeet Reservation to help start the project in a good way. Ten people took part in this event and agreed that the project had potential to present an authentic view of Blackfeet people and their relationship with the mountains. All present chose to set aside the difficult political situation that exists between the Blackfeet and Glacier Park because of the loss of the important traditional areas on the east side of the park and, for this book, to focus on the rich traditions that come from the mountains and that remain the fundamental underpinnings of Blackfeet culture.

Constructive dialogue during these gatherings was essential to establishing a collaborative working relationship and an understanding of how the book project would serve everyone involved in beneficial ways. We began a tentative process of working together. My job was to compile everything I could find in the written record—from the oral histories of the Kootenai and the Blackfeet as told by their ancestors to explorers, adventurers, anthropologists, and historians over the last two centuries— and from interviews on the seasonal rounds of both tribes and to organize this information and prepare the manuscript, which the tribal representatives would revise.

A significant change happened once the tribal committees understood that *they* were the authors of their respective chapters in the book. They stepped forward to contribute and took the time needed to thoughtfully correct misperceptions that have always found their way into writings of outside observers. Accuracy took on a new dimension since this effort was for themselves and their grandchildren as much as it was for park visitors.

Each group defined the parameters of what would be shared. Because of the differences between these two cultures, their resulting chapters are distinct. The Blackfeet chose to include a major section on their ceremonies and how they dictate the activities of their seasonal round, whereas the Kootenais chose to explain their worldview as it is informed through their spiritual teachings while keeping their ceremonial practices to themselves. The Blackfeet committee noted that way too much emphasis has been placed on warfare, so this book includes stories of peace-making, examples of cooperation, and protocols for entering the territory of another.

The process of coauthoring this book has been life-changing for me. After working with American Indian and First Nations communities for more than twenty years, I am beginning to realize that my biases, no matter how conscious of them I try to become, have always dominated the way I navigate the research landscape. Working together in balanced partnerships such as these recognizes what we have to offer one another. In this project, I contributed research skills to locate and contextualize materials held in archives. The tribal representatives reviewed, added information, and made corrections to reclaim tribal knowledge. Information from previous authors included in this work has been corrected, as appropriate, by the tribal representatives. The Kootenai team accepts that what is here is "good enough for now" but wants it acknowledged that the information here relies heavily on documented information from previous authors who have been intentionally fed misinformation by less-than-cooperative informants. As a result of this experience, each of us recognized that the tribal nations are the only ones who have the right to determine what they want to share with outsiders.

Our intention here is to draw attention to the rich relationships these two tribes had, and continue to have, with the mountains, glaciers, rivers, lakes, and all the life supported by them in what is now Glacier National Park. To enter the pre-park world, it's important to suspend what you think you know about Indians and the park. Much of that mystique was created as part of a marketing blitz by the Great Northern Railway to attract people to Glacier. With a quarter century of Winold Reiss's portraits of Blackfeet men and women, along with tipi encampments occupied by Blackfeet in full regalia dancing for visitors at the lodges, it is no wonder that people have a stereotypical view of Blackfeet people and the park. And very few people know of the strong connection and rich history the Kootenais have in relation to Glacier Park.

This book is an opportunity for readers to learn from Native inhabitants about their histories within these mountain lands. It's an attempt to carry the reader through their seasons with a sense of the feel of the crunching snow on a cold winter day and the smell of sap running in spring. Most of all, we hope you'll hear the laughter of children and the soothing voices of their elders as they tell the old stories of life in and around the mountains of Glacier Park.

Acknowledgments

◈

Thıs book is a beginning. It has taken many people to compile, organize, and reconcile the information provided through archival sources and to expound on these re-creations of traditional seasonal rounds from oral histories and life experiences.

I want to commend Jack Potter for his leadership in cross-cultural work in the park. But my thanks go to so many others. The Kootenai Culture Committee (KCC), based in Elmo, Montana, took the lead for their chapter. Patricia Hewankorn, KCC director, assigned Vernon Finley, director of their Language Curriculum Project, to coordinate the effort. Vernon has a gift for translating traditional Kootenai beliefs and perspectives into English and into an American worldview. His contributions were significant. With good humor, he helped me through many rough spots in the process. Naida Lefthand was given the responsibility to oversee the Kootenai content. Naida patiently worked with me to explain Kootenai perspectives so that we could use the right words to accurately represent the brilliant lifeway of her ancestors. I am grateful for the care that she took to help us create something that corrects some misperceptions from the past and that will serve well into the future.

Reflections on the continuation of cultural values were generously provided by two granddaughters of the last chief of the Ksanka Band, Margaret Friedlander and Cathy Hamel. Cathy's daughter, Gigi Caye, facilitated this process. I am grateful to all three for their insights. I also want to thank Francis Auld, Sadie Saloway, Helen Charlo, Lucy Caye, Matt Michel, Louise Andrew, Catherine Andrew, Ignace Couture, and all the elders who contributed their thoughts at KCC meetings during this three-year process. The staff of the KCC, including Gina Big Beaver, Gigi Caye, Rosemary Caye, Susan Antiste, and Dorothy Berney, were always helpful in assisting with the process. I want to thank Tim Ryan for his particularly generous sharing of his extensive knowledge of the plants that were—and are—used to construct tools, containers, clothing, and shelters, and for images of his authentic reproductions.

In addition to the Ksanka Band, many people from the Tobacco Plains and St. Mary Bands in British Columbia contributed content and suggestions, including Liz Gravelle, Leo Williams, Laura Birdstone, Dorothy Alpine, Herman Alpine, Jon and Mary Mahseelah, Hazel Pascal, Jenny Alpine, Patsy Nicholas, and Pauline Eugene. Margaret Teneese helped to review historical photographs for use in the book.

Many Kootenai elders from earlier generations have contributed to the preservation of the oral histories from which this book derives. We honor them for their knowledge, wisdom, and generosity.

I am extremely grateful for the guidance provided for the Blackfeet sections of the book by Smokey and Darnell Rides At The Door. They coordinated and hosted several gatherings to bring together broad-based perspectives from various bands of Pikunni and spent many hours helping me to understand the fine points of Blackfeet culture. In addition to their knowledge, I am grateful for their kindness, generosity, patience, and friendship. Other contributors include G. G. and Melinda Kipp, Cynthia Kipp, Edmond "Wishie" and Arlene Augare, Peter "Rusty" and Lorrie Tatsey, Molly and Marilyn Bullshoe, Leo Bird, Pauline Matt, Calvin Weatherwax, Roy Doore Jr., and Bob and Charlene Burns. Linda Juneau, Iris Heavy Runner Pretty Paint, and Patty LaPlant have been important teachers of traditional lifeways. From their neighbors to the north, the Kainai, I was assisted in this project by Narcisse Blood, Frank Weasel Head, and Peter and Deloras Weasel Moccasin. I also want to thank the Blackfeet Tribal Council for their support of the project.

One of the most important learning experiences for me during the writing process was working with students at Browning High School. The students helped me to understand that paintings of their ancestors created by outsiders carry cultural biases, no matter how much the artists tried to illustrate faithfully what they observed. Working together to share what we perceived through these images was transformational. I am grateful to all the students who participated and to Lorrie Tatsey for coordinating the visits.

Many Blackfeet elders from earlier generations have offered their knowledge to anthropologists and historians, helping to preserve knowledge of lifeways no longer possible. I was fortunate to work with many of these cultural leaders on earlier projects, and I am grateful for the opportunity to have learned from them. Their wisdom is threaded throughout the book.

This book required familiarity with the plants, animals, and geography of Glacier National Park, much of which I didn't know. Many kind people have helped to expand my knowledge and to check the results for errors. Natural history content was improved by valuable contributions made by botanist Peter Lesica and educator and naturalist Christine Wren. Peter reviewed all the botanical references in the manuscript, provided additional sources, and contributed photographs. Christine has read through the original manuscript more times than anyone but me, bringing her fine-toothed comb to the editing process. In addition, she contributed many details about the nesting habits of birds and other pieces of natural history that greatly enhance the book. Ken Furrow's knowledge of wildlife is extensive, and he has shared generously with me through many years of traveling back roads together while on film shoots. Darris Flanagan loaned me all of his research materials, accumulated over many years, on Kootenai trails, as did Duke Hoiland. Their kindness is greatly appreciated. Jack and Rachel Potter helped make sense of many geographical particulars, drawing on their rich knowledge of every trail in Glacier. Tara Carolin organized a well-attended brown-bag presentation with park personnel, which helped to refine the content of the book. I appreciate all of the input from this session. Historian William E. Farr kindly read through a draft, drawing on his extensive knowledge of this era to help refine the particulars.

Many individuals and organizations contributed photographs to this book. I want to especially thank Kimberly Lugthart for sourcing so many of the images to help bring these stories to life. Thanks also to Bryony Schwan for her generous contribution of her spectacular image of birds in flight over Freezeout Lake.

This book would never have happened without three key people from Glacier Park. Lon Johnson has overseen the project through a much longer and more circuitous route than ever imagined, and all in good humor. His knowledge and experience regarding the tribal communities and their cultural resources as well as the historical resources relevant to the project have significantly contributed to the outcome. Deirdre

Shaw helped sort through the archival resources of the park and assisted with finding illustrations to help bring the story to life. Her extensive knowledge of these resources has been a significant contribution to the book. Finally, Jack Potter had the original idea for the book as a centennial project, and he unfailingly supported the roundabout and sometimes challenging evolution of the effort. I hope the results meet his expectations.

Gay Allison and Ric Hauer of the University of Montana's NSF-EPSCoR office recognized the significance of this project and generously contributed funding to support the gathering of Kootenai elders at Yellow Bay. The University of Montana's biological station, directed by Jack Stanford, provided the space for the event. The support provided by both University of Montana entities is gratefully acknowledged.

Working with the team at the Montana Historical Society Press has been such a great pleasure. With the visionary leadership of Molly Holz and manuscript editor Ursula Smith, the manuscript has been transformed into a much improved book. Glenda Bradshaw understood the imperative for well-placed photographs to visually tell a cyclical story, and Diane Gleba Hall transformed the pages into this beautiful design. Christy Eckerle worked on various aspects of the effort, especially promotion. I am grateful to them all, and thank them for their careful midwifing of this creation.

Many friends and family members took time to listen and help with various aspects of the research, writing, and editing process. Thanks to each and every one. I especially want to thank Joyce Hocker for inspiring the focus on cultural continuity and resilience in the final chapter. From start to finish, this was a true collaboration.

Just as the book was going to press, I received the terrible news of the car accident that took Narcisse Blood's life. I want to acknowledge how much Narcisse influenced and contributed to all the work I have done for the last fifteen years. He was an inspiring and exceptional man who gave generously of his traditional cultural knowledge to so many people. I dedicate this book to his memory.

—Sally Thompson

People Before the Park

▸ ▸ ▸ ▸ ▸ ▸ ▸ ◈ ◂ ◂ ◂ ◂ ◂ ◂ ◂

The Continental Divide in Glacier National Park is variously called the Crown of the Continent and the Backbone of the World. T. J. Hileman, photographer, Glacier National Park, 4186

Chapter 1

◈

The Land That Is Glacier National Park

by Sally Thompson

Picture the continent of North America. Imagine twenty-eight thousand square miles of wild, mountainous terrain that serves as a last refuge for the mammals, birds, fish, and plants that once thrived in the region. Glacier National Park now makes up a significant part of this bioregion known as the Crown of the Continent. From Glacier's peaks flow the headwaters for the Missouri to the Mississippi, the Saskatchewan to Hudson's Bay, and the Flathead to the Columbia. Triple Divide Peak marks this sacred center.

Approached from the east, Glacier Park rises dramatically from windswept plains. Spectacular rocky peaks of red, white, and gray emerge from expansive rolling grasslands, each layer taller than the one before. The glaciers, at least what remains of them and their turquoise-blue waters, provide sharp contrast to the surrounding landscape. The Sweet Grass Hills, nearly one hundred miles away, are visible on a clear day.

Approached from the west, curving narrow canyons of steep conifer-green slopes straddle intermountain creeks and rivers. Ancient cedars thrive here. Awe-inspiring peaks rise from the shores of the long, narrow lakes of the North Fork Valley. Carved by glaciers, these lakes serve as gateways to some of the most rugged terrain in the park.

The interior of the park is difficult to access. Each year the famous Going-to-the-Sun Road requires repair from avalanches and rockslides. Once on top, highline trails carry summer travelers into some of the most beautiful alpine country imaginable. Snowmelt waterfalls pour over cliff walls. Wildflowers explode at the edge of the retreating snow, as if they know how short the season might be. All four seasons can be compressed into a month.

The land we call Glacier today is but a fraction of the size of the region the indigenous peoples once called home. The Kootenai tell a creation story that alludes to a homeland much larger than the Flathead Reservation and the small reserves in Canada to which the Kootenais are confined today. Theirs was a homeland that stretched from what is now Yellowstone National Park all the way to Yellowhead Pass near Jasper in the Canadian Rockies.

Kootenai Creation Story

LONG, long ago, in ancestral times, the chief animal, Nalmuqcin, called a council to determine what could be done about the water monster, Yawu'nik. Despite Nalmuqcin's enormous size—he had to crawl on hands and knees to keep from hitting his head on the ceiling of the sky—he couldn't capture Yawu'nik.

After chasing around in the lands that would become home to the Kootenai people, a wise old one named Kikum told Nalmuqcin to quit wasting his time chasing the monster and instead to block the flow of the river with one sweep of his massive arm, thus creating a lake where he could trap Yawu'nik. And this he did.

Red-headed Woodpecker was given the honor of killing Yawu'nik, after which Nalmuqcin distributed the monster's body parts far and wide. These became the lands where the different races of people would be created. Where he wiped the blood from his hands was where the red people would remain forever.

Nalmuqcin was so happy to be rid of the monster that he stood upright, hitting his head on the ceiling of the sky. With that he dropped down, dead. His feet went northward to the area of Yellowhead Pass, near Jasper in the Canadian Rockies, and his head ended up near Yellowstone Park in Montana. His body then became the Rocky Mountains.

—Ktunaxa traditional story[1]

Before the jagged mountain crest of the Continental Divide—the "Backbone of the World"—was contained within a national park, the peaks and valleys, lakes, and rivers on the east side of the divide belonged to the Blackfeet, or, as the Blackfeet themselves would say, *they* belonged

Old Man and the Great Spirit

▸ ▸ ▸ ▸ ▸ ▸ ▸ ◈ ◂ ◂ ◂ ◂ ◂ ◂ ◂

THERE was once a Great Spirit who was good. He made a man and a woman. Then the Old Man came along. No one made Old Man; he always existed. The Great Spirit said to him, "Old Man, have you any power?" "Yes," said Old Man, "I am very strong." "Well," said the Great Spirit, "suppose you make some mountains." So Old Man set to work and made the Sweet-Grass Hills. To do this he took a piece of Chief Mountain. He brought Chief Mountain up to its present location, shaped it up, and named it. The other mountains were called blood clots. "Well," said the Great Spirit, "You are strong."

—Excerpted from Wissler and Duvall, *Mythology of the Blackfoot Indians*, 23

to the mountains and prairies. Blackfeet oral history, like that of the Kootenai, contains a creation story that illustrates the expanse of their homeland long before the federal government established their reservation. It is a story set in a cultural landscape stretching eastward from the Continental Divide to north-central Montana and southern Alberta. Its principal landmarks are Chief Mountain on the Rocky Mountain Front and the Sweet Grass Hills to the east.

Times have changed in this area of the Rocky Mountains over the last century. Let your mind wander back to a time before logging changed so much of the landscape and imagine old-growth forests on the west side of the Continental Divide, with tamaracks 13 feet in circumference and 150 feet to the first branch. Picture small caribou herds in winter, eating the mosses that thrived in old cedar groves. Imagine the east-side parklands along the mountain edge covered with buffalo as winter arrived and with ground-nesting birds in spring so thick travelers found it a challenge not to step on one.

In those days, prairies were more extensive due to the diligent burning practices of the tribes on both sides of the Continental Divide. In fact, according to the Confederated Salish and Kootenai Tribes, this area "was a cultural landscape, a landscape in which the plant and animal communities had been shaped in large part by many thousands of years of burning by Indian people."[2] Where now aspen groves rim the mountain prairies, once were open grasslands. Where lodgepoles now crowd out the sunlight, huckleberries once grew in sweet abundance.

In these homelands, moon cycles organized time, year after year. By observing the revolving seasons over the generations, indigenous people came to have a collective knowledge of life within the territory. By watching the moon and stars, and by sensing the signs that presage a change of season—hearing the first thunder, observing ermine losing their winter white, and smelling the sap running in the trees—people came to anticipate the first foods of spring. When the sun had cycled halfway through its journey, subtle changes in wind direction, quality of hides, and animal behavior would indicate when the cold would return. Patterns were predictable, and each moon would tell the people where they were in the flow of life within the revolving seasons of their homeland.

Those of us who rely on clocks and calendars will have to suspend our need for a history that can be plugged into a timeline. Instead, we will have to assume the indigenous people's sense of time as we move through their age-old stories.

Chapter 2

◈

The Tribes of the
Glacier National Park Area

BY SALLY THOMPSON

WHEN Glacier National Park was created in 1910, it was not a wilderness to the people who had long lived in and around these mountains. This book focuses on the two tribes whose traditional territories include what is now the park: the Kootenai on the west side and the Blackfeet on the east. These two tribes have strong continuing connections to the area, but they are not the only tribes to have spent time during the nineteenth century in and around the land that was to become Glacier. For example, Stony Pass, in the north-central area of the park, is named for the Stony Nation to the north, whose people entered the area to hunt. Pend d'Oreille territory included mountains to the south of Glacier. They, along with the Salish, the Cree, and the Métis, also moved in and out of the region.

General locations of the Kootenai and Blackfeet in relation to what is now Glacier National Park

You are invited into the world of the Kootenais and the Blackfeet to learn about their relationships with the places that are now within

Glacier and the surrounding areas. These relationships are distinctive. The Kootenais' homeland and cultural practices dictate one reality and the Blackfeet's another. From different directions and with different intentions, these tribes entered the mountains year after year as part of their seasonal rounds.

Although both tribes have long histories in the region, this book focuses on the century before Glacier Park was established, since details of life during this period are available both through oral histories and written accounts, while earlier times have left a less tangible record.

The Kootenai

Originally, the Kootenais were 'Aqɬsmaknik, the People. The people known as Kootenais in the United States are known in Canada as Ktunaxa (pronounced k-too-nah-ha). The Kootenais of the Confederated Salish and Kootenai Nation in Montana identify themselves as the Ksanka (pronounced k-san-ka) Band, or "People of the Standing Arrow," referring to qualities of strength, unity, and dexterity.[1]

Kootenais, wherever found, are a unique people, with a language like no other. Although they share a reservation with the Salish and Pend d'Oreille, the American Kootenais are not related linguistically to these Salishan-speakers. The source of the name "Kootenai" is unclear. The names of tribes were generally given by their neighbors and described some distinguishing characteristic. Several signs for Kootenai in Plains Indian Sign Language demonstrate this pattern: "People of the White-Tail Deer," "Canoe People," "Water People," and "Fish Eaters." One Blackfeet sign for the Kootenais means "People-Who-Live-In-The-Mountains."[2]

Kootenai groups are known by their locations. As their populations declined through time, the Kootenais coalesced into seven contemporary bands. These include bands living in British Columbia—the Columbia Lake Band (Windermere); the St. Mary Band (Cranbrook); the Tobacco Plains Band (Grasmere); the Lower Kootenay (Creston); and the Shuswap Band (Invermere). On the U.S. side of the border are the Bonner's Ferry Band in Idaho and the Ksanka Band based in Elmo, Montana.

The bands most associated with the mountains around Glacier Park during the nineteenth century were the Tobacco Plains Band and the Ksanka Band. As reported to anthropologist Claude Schaeffer, who worked among the Kootenais in the 1930s through the 1960s:

Woman with Kootenai elk hide canoe, 1910 E. S. Curtis, photographer, Library of Congress, LC-USZ62-47004

The Tobacco Plains group is called akanahonek. This was the name for a certain length, about a mile, of the mouth of a small creek running into Grave Creek (a tributary of the Tobacco River). The meaning of akanaho is "the current." This was the original home of the band.

Akanahonek territory seems to have varied considerably in direction and extent during the last century and a half, increasing or diminishing according to changes of economy. Before the adoption of bison hunting in the eastern foothills of the Rockies, the activities of the band seem to have been largely confined to the area within the main Kootenay River Valley and its major affluents, and the Continental Divide, the western forested foothills of the latter serving as the principal hunting region. Only infrequently did hunting parties cross the Kootenai River westward and then only to secure caribou in the nearby mountains.[3]

Anthropologists claim that, in the early nineteenth century, the Jennings Band, referred to historically by the Kootenais as Akiyinik, a name referring to some small meadows, shifted their territory southeastward, around the north end of Flathead Lake. With this move, they increased their buffalo-hunting activities and their use of what is now Glacier Park and the Bob Marshall Wilderness to the south. But late in the nineteenth century, with growing numbers of Euro-American immigrants settling in

The Archaeological Evidence

ARCHAEOLOGICAL evidence of Native peoples in the park dates back thousands of years, to the end of the Late Pleistocene, as evidenced by lanceolate projectile points found near the confluence of the headwaters of the Flathead River. Distinctive cultural practices are evidenced by archaeological remains within the traditional territories of the two tribes, Kootenai and Blackfeet. For example, the Blackfeet used only particular types of rocks for sweat lodges, selected for their heat-holding and nonfracturing characteristics. Clusters of these rock features show continuity in this practice for well over two thousand years. Fasting beds, also known as vision quest sites, are also common in high places on the east side, coinciding with stories shared about quests for spirit helpers throughout Blackfeet history. Kootenais sought visions as well, but the archaeological evidence of their quests is less well known. However, places in and around the west side, and on the east side as well, hold indications of this important spiritual activity.[4]

Stones used for grinding berries and pounding meat have been recovered from many old campsites on both sides of Glacier, particularly

The Kootenais stored preserved foods separately in skin bags, like the reproductions seen here, or in cedar boxes. Courtesy Tim Ryan

in the North Fork valleys and around Waterton, St. Mary, Two Medicine, Many Glacier, and up Cutbank Canyon. These stone tools vary stylistically and functionally depending on the Blackfeet and Kootenai cultural context.[5]

For the Blackfeet, meat was dried, packed, and stored in large parfleches—containers made of tough rawhide that were folded in the form of a suitcase. Dried berries were kept in skin or hoof bags. In addition to processing dry meat, the Blackfeet ground meat, berries, and fat together to make pemmican, a food for traveling purposes. In contrast, the west side groups—the Kootenai, Pend d'Oreille, and Salish—didn't grind meat with berries or roots. Their foods were processed separately and kept in separate skin bags or cedar boxes for storage and later consumption.

In addition to the presence of grinding stones around the edges of old campsites, another archaeological indicator of Kootenais in the North Fork area of Glacier is found in the form of scarred ponderosa pines that provided cambium, a traditional food source, rich in carbohydrates. This inner bark was harvested in the springtime, providing a sweet treat after the long winter.[6]

Stone maul and pestle found on the shores of Lake McDonald Malouf, Carling. "Pestles." *Archaeology In Montana* 4 (4): 3–6. 1962

the area, the Akiyinik coalesced in the Big Arm Bay area of Flathead Lake around Dayton, Elmo, and Big Arm. The Akiyinik were joined there by many Lower Kootenai, historically associated with the Lower Kootenai River.[7] These people now are collectively known as the Ksanka Band. However, the Ksankas recognize all of the area between Nalmuqcin's head (Yellowstone) and feet (Yellowhead Pass) as territory they utilized in their yearly cycle of hunting and gathering.

The Blackfeet

The Blackfeet are part of the extensive world of Algonquian-speakers. Although linguists argue about the motherland of these tribes and the center from which they spread, the Blackfeet say they've always lived in the region, claiming, "All of our history and our creation are within this area—the mountains, the plains."[8]

The modern Blackfoot Confederacy consists of the North Piegan (Aapátohsi Pikunni); the South Piegan (Aamsskáápi Pikunni), who are known as Blackfeet in Montana; the Blood (Káínai); and the Siksika, also known as the Blackfoot. The South Piegan, generally referred to here as Pikunni, are located in Montana, and the other three tribes are located in Alberta. Together they call themselves the Niitsítapi (the "Original People").[9]

You may have read that people don't remember how the Blackfeet got their name. Some say that another group observed them walking across some scorched earth that turned their moccasins black, and that's how they got their name. According to their own oral tradition, the name "Blackfeet" was given to the oldest son of a Nitsitaapi leader long, long ago, to acknowledge the "secret black medicine on his son's feet which enabled him to run right up alongside a band of the animals [buffalo] and kill a number of them with bow and arrow." "My son," the father said, "you have done a great favor to us all. I see now that we are to become a very numerous people; too many to all camp together and hunt together. Therefore, you and your children, and those to come after them, shall be known as the Blackfeet clan. In time to come you must leave us, and choose, and live in a part of this great hunting ground Old Man has given us."[10]

The two younger brothers were jealous, so their father told them to go in search of new lands for their growing numbers and he would give them names according to what they experienced on their travels. The middle son was given the name Pikunni, or "Spotted Robes," referring to beautiful clothing that he had captured during his travels. The youngest son became Ahk-kaina, referring to the "Many Chiefs" he killed in his travels. This latter band is mistakenly known today as "Bloods."[11]

The population of the collective groups of Blackfeet at one time numbered in the tens of thousands, organized in bands of several hundred each. Like the Kootenai, beginning in the mid-eighteenth century, they suffered massive losses through smallpox and other diseases and warfare. Then, in the late nineteenth century, they lost hundreds of people to starvation. With each wave of loss, people regrouped, constellating into a smaller number of bands.

During the nineteenth century, the westernmost bands of the Pikunni had the closest relationship to the area that would become Glacier National Park, especially after the treaties of the midcentury. The southwestern

The Blackfeet came together in council with the Gros Ventre, Nez Perce, Pend d'Oreille, Flathead, and one Cree to negotiate the Lame Bull Treaty of 1855. Blackfoot Council, by Gustavus Sohon, Washington State Historical Society, Tacoma, 1918.114.9.1

bands of the Blood, or Kainai, and the Northern Piegan also had strong relationships with these mountains, especially in the Waterton area.

Before the treaties, the east side of Glacier and Waterton Lakes National Parks was part of a seamless Blackfeet homeland providing the foods, supplies, and spiritual sustenance required for their way of life. The establishment of reservations for the Pikunni in the United States and Canada and the Kainai in Canada—the 1855 Lame Bull Treaty in the States and 1877 Treaty Seven in Canada—and the encroachment of non-Indian settlements to their east and south, intensified the Indians' relationship with the mountains. This connection grew even stronger after the extermination of the buffalo in the 1880s, as the mountains provided elk, deer, moose, sheep, and other animals for food and clothing. With the creation of Glacier in 1910, the Pikunni had to shift their focus to the mountains south of the park, on lands administered by the Lewis and Clark National Forest, where their off-reservation treaty rights still apply.

Relationships between the Tribes

Anthropologists and historians have emphasized warfare in their recounting of tribal histories in this region. Despite ample evidence of alliances, shared hunts, intermarriage, and trade, scholars tend to focus their attention on battles, making it difficult to ascertain the relative influence and frequency of warfare versus times of peace. This is not to say that conflicts weren't common; they were.

Pressures resulting from the fur trade were already felt decades before the first white men arrived in the territories of the Kootenai and Blackfeet. Before Native peoples ever saw whites, they had already experienced the arrival of horses, guns, and epidemics. Horses, captured from tribes to the south in the early to mid-eighteenth century, expanded the distances that could be traveled and changed the strategies for hunting buffalo. With this new method of transportation, more people entered the buffalo plains, and they traveled there with greater frequency, creating more opportunities for conflict among tribes. As competition increased, the Blackfeet defended the buffalo plains of their homeland from intruders, leading at times to warfare.

Another significant factor that altered the balance of power was the acquisition of guns by the Blackfeet from Cree traders in the late eighteenth century, some two decades before the Kootenais were armed by the Hudson's Bay Company. Rifles changed warfare as well as hunting strategies. Before rifles, warfare had more often been a means to demonstrate bravery through counting coups. Young men could prove themselves by sneaking into a camp and capturing horses or by touching a famous enemy warrior with their coup stick. The competition was less about killing and more about skill and courage. But once rifles became commonplace, so did killing.

The Ravages of Smallpox

▶ ▶ ▶ ▶ ▶ ▶ ▶   ◈   ◀ ◀ ◀ ◀ ◀ ◀ ◀

THE spring of 1837 brought another devastating round of smallpox, carried upriver by steamboat. Major Alexander Culbertson, a fur trader and mountain man, tried to keep the Piegans and Bloods who were camped by the fort from coming aboard the ship, but they were eager to trade and were unable to understand the consequences. Exposed to this dreaded disease, they returned to their family camps, carrying the enemy within them. After two months without contact with the Blackfeet, Culbertson headed to their usual late summer camp area at the Three Forks to learn for himself what had happened. Many years later, after an 1870 interview with Culbertson, Lieutenant James Bradley described the scene:

> A few days travel brought him in sight of a village of about sixty lodges. Not a soul was to be seen, and a funereal stillness rested upon it. They approached with anxious hearts and awed by the unwonted quiet, for the vicinity of an Indian village is not apt to be the scene of oppressive silence. Soon a stench was observed in the air, that increased as they advanced; and presently the scene with all its horror was before them. Hundreds of decaying forms of human beings, horses and dogs lay scattered everywhere among the lodges. . . . Two old women, too feeble to travel, were the sole living occupants of the village.

> —From Bradley, "Affairs at Fort Benton," 221–22, 225

Death from epidemics resulted in some territorial shifts and reconstellation of bands. Over the period of three centuries, as many as 80 percent of indigenous Americans died from European diseases. One band of Kootenais was nearly wiped out by smallpox during this precontact period. Their absence allowed the Kainai to take over this Kootenai home territory around Waterton Lakes. Every tribe has its story of the horrors of smallpox, as shown on the winter-count calendar of one band of Blackfeet.[12]

Winter count symbol for 1837, the year of smallpox Paul M. Raczka, *Winter Count: A History of the Blackfoot People* (Brocket, Alta.: Oldman River Cultural Centre, 1979), 45

We have lost sight of the fact that many tribal stories tell about events that happened and things that were learned in exchanges between the Kootenais and the Blackfeet as they visited each other's camps. Inter-marriage was another mechanism for establishing social and trade relationships between bands in the days before non-Indians arrived. These details don't generally make it into the history books because they are simply part of the normal flow of life. Fortunately, some examples of intertribal cooperation were told in passing, such as the story of how Mountain Chief found his horses. James Willard Schultz, an adventurer and writer who came west as an eighteen-year-old in 1877 and married into the Blackfeet tribe, recorded the story told him by Yellow Wolf about a time when the Bloods were hunting along Cutbank Creek in the company of a Kootenai visitor.

"At one time," Schultz wrote,

> the Bloods, along with their Kootenai visitor, were hunting along Cutbank Creek, "every day or two moving closer and closer to the mountains." Mountain Chief, the leader of the band, became aware that two of his best horses were missing, and he sent young men to look for them. The main camp kept moving their location closer to the mountains and eventually found themselves camped at the edge of the mountains (close to where there is now a campground in Glacier). The Kootenai visitor approached the chief and offered to help him find the missing horses.[13]

> When Mountain Chief agreed, the Kootenai medicine man instructed Mountain Chief to give him "a robe, a good bow, and a quiver of arrows," then told him to call in the leading men of the camp, which Mountain Chief did. The Kootenai then taught them a sacred song, "a call to all living things. It was low in tone, and slow; a strange and beautiful song that gripped one's heart."

> Then the Kootenai told Mountain Chief to have the women build for him a little lodge there inside the big lodge. "Into this little enclosure crept the Kootenai, taking with him a bird

Mountain Chief, Blackfeet Mountain Chief, by Gustavus Sohon,
Washington State Historical Society, Tacoma, 1918.114.9.26

wing-bone whistle and a medicine rattle," and as soon as he was inside, he instructed the people to sing the sacred song four times.

Now the Kootenai, alone in his dark little lodge, sang another song, keeping time to it with his rattle, and the people heard the sighing of the wind through a big pine tree, although no such tree was near; and the Kootenai questioned the pine tree, and it answered that it had no knowledge of the missing horses.

Others followed, the different birds and the animals; one could hear outside the flutter of their wings, the tread of their feet; and the Kootenai questioned them, and one by one they answered that they had not seen the horses.

The Kootenai called the people to sing the sacred song again, four times more. He blew his whistle and, although the wind had not been blowing, "soon they heard, far off, the roar of an approaching wind of terrible force." Even Old-Man-of-the-Winds did not know about the missing horses, but said that his friend, Red-Top Plume, who lived in the clouds and could see the whole country, would be able to help. The Kootenai was told to "Watch the clouds. When you see one of them turning from white to red as the sun goes down . . . , you will know that Red-Top Plume is there above you."

The Kootenai, still in his dark little lodge, told Mountain Chief to go outside and watch. Mountain Chief looked up and saw four small clouds drift together to form one. Soon the edge of the cloud began to turn red. With that, the people joined the chief in singing the song four times. Then the Kootenai blew his wing-bone whistle.

After a period of anxious silence, they all heard a deep and beautiful voice. "I am Red-Top Plume! Why have you called me here?" The Kootenai told him of the lost black horses and asked if he had seen them. "That is a small thing to call me down about . . . but since I am here, I will tell you what I know: Yes, I have seen them. . . . They are standing beside the spring just up the hill from where you camped when you lost them."

The people were amazed, and the Kootenai cried out, "Red-Top Plume! You are good to us. What we can do for you?" But Red-Top Plume was gone, moving slowly eastward, his beautiful plumes redder than ever.

And while the Kootenai and Mountain Chief and the other warriors made sacrifice to him, some young men mounted their horses and rode back to the camping place where the two horses had been lost, and lo! they found them near the spring where Red-Top Plume had said they were standing.

The Blackfeet have stories about trade relationships and the protocols to follow when meeting another tribe. There was a ceremony for how to behave with each other. According to G. G. Kipp, "When we enter new territory, the song is the same song that we sing when we raise the center pole for the Okan [Medicine Lodge]. We'd stand on a hill and we'd announce ourselves. 'We're coming. We're coming in a peaceful way.'"[14]

The Kootenais followed much the same protocol in coming into another tribe's camp. In 1862, Bear Necklace, a Kootenai chief, asked permission of the Kainai to winter in the foothills east of the mountains.[15] Bear Necklace and the Kainais' chief smoked the pipe and Bear Necklace's band spent the winter on the St. Mary River. The winter was spent in peaceful relations, with the Kootenais and Kainai enjoying games, gambling, and storytelling together. Eventually, a stolen racehorse led to bloodshed and the end of the peace. But too often we only hear of the bloodshed and forget the times spent in good relations.

These old protocols for respectfully entering the territory of another tribe are still acknowledged, as evidenced by a recent story, as told by G. G. Kipp:

Conrad Lafromboise made a special trip over to see Johnny Arlee, a spiritual leader on the Flathead, to ask, "Is it okay if I come into your country and pray at that school?" Johnny says, "Sure, you feel welcome to." That was traditional protocol. Because that was their area—their territory—and that practice is something that has happened for centuries. In return, they would come over to visit us, and say, "We come over maybe to get food, maybe to do something. We're going to be in your country for a month." And we'd tell them, "Go ahead. There's plenty for all. Travel, take this and take that."[16]

Such stories reveal a different, more nuanced and interesting history of the relationships among the various bands of Blackfeet and Kootenais than do the tired old war stories.

Chapter 3

◈

The Coming of White Men

by Sally Thompson

THE Canadian fur trade reached the Blackfeet and the Kootenais before the arrival of Lewis and Clark in the West in 1805–1806. In fact, as early as October 1754, Anthony Henday of the Hudson's Bay Company arrived at a Kainai camp on the Saskatchewan River. By 1779, the North West and Hudson's Bay Companies had set up rival posts on the North Saskatchewan River, just east of the Continental Divide in the territory of the northernmost Blackfoot tribe, the Siksika. Trading with other bands in those early years was worked through a network using Cree traders as middlemen. But by the 1790s, the Canadian fur trade was seeking locations in Blackfeet territory for establishing posts.

In 1792, Peter Fidler, also in the employ of the Hudson's Bay Company, made mention of the Kootenais—"Cotton-na-haws"—in his journal. Both the Hudson's Bay and the North West Companies hoped to establish fur trade on the west side of the divide, but that goal was largely thwarted by the Blackfeet until July 1806, when Meriwether Lewis's party killed two adolescent boys on the Two Medicine River. At that point, the Blackfeet turned their attention against American traders to the southeast, creating an opportunity for the North West Company, led by David Thompson, to slip across the Continental Divide and establish Kootenay House on the Upper Columbia.[1]

The establishment of a post in the territory of the Kootenais created more equality in Native access to European products, especially armaments, which, in turn, incited an increase in warfare between the Blackfeet and the tribes west of the Continental Divide—the Kootenai, Pend d'Oreille, and Salish.

The Fur Trade

Competition among rival international corporations for fur-bearing animals of North America began soon after Europeans first landed on the East Coast. The French were strong in the early trade in the East until the French and Indian War, after which the British dominated. It was during these years at the close of the eighteenth century that fur traders, along with French voyageurs and Iroquois trappers, expanded their territories into the Rocky Mountains.

Americans were soon struggling to gain a foothold in the Northwest, but they were unable to effectively compete, especially after the North West Company was subsumed by the Hudson's Bay Company in 1821, making the latter one of the largest commercial firms in the world. Fort Vancouver on the Columbia River became the center for the Columbia Department of the Hudson's Bay Company, which included all of the Northwest, from Russian Alaska to Spanish California and from the Pacific Coast to the Rocky Mountains. At the height of operations, twenty-three forts were located within the Columbia Department.

Beaver was the principal species sought by fur traders in the Rockies because the pelts, pressed into felt, were used to make men's hats, which were the rage in Europe. This trade, involving some one hundred thousand beaver pelts per year, required participation by Native peoples as trappers, as trading partners, and as wives. The Blackfeet and Kootenai responded very differently to the fur trade. The Kootenais, who traditionally trapped fur-bearing animals for clothing, became actively engaged in bringing beaver pelts to the trade houses, a practice that intensified their use of remote river tributaries. The Blackfeet, on the other hand, with their close spiritual relationship to the beaver, chose not to trap these brothers for commercial purposes but opted instead to provide buffalo robes to the Canadian traders.[2]

Escalated warring was the backdrop for the decades when the fur trade flourished, all the more so as beaver pelts, buffalo robes, and other trade goods became more and more scarce, heightening competition between

Early Contact with Europeans

▶ ▶ ▶ ▶ ▶ ▶ ▶ ◈ ◀ ◀ ◀ ◀ ◀ ◀ ◀

IN October 1754 hundreds of Kainais watched Anthony Henday and his Cree guides enter their camp on the Saskatchewan River and walk through the esplanade created by two hundred tipis, pitched in two long parallel rows.

The horses, tethered to the lodges, whinnied as these strangers walked among them. From the great lodge at the end of the street, the chief and twenty elders waited for their visitors. Inside the lodge, the strangers were seated next to the chief. The pipe was passed around in silence, and then willow baskets full of boiled buffalo tongue were shared. After these formalities were completed, Henday told the men of his purpose and invited the chief to send young men to Hudson's Bay to exchange their furs for rifles, tobacco, blankets, ammunition, colored cloth, and beads.

The chief waited politely for the interpreter to complete his signing of the message, then told the visitor how the Blackfeet were horsemen, not accustomed to canoes; they ate meat, not fish; and they had heard about Indians who starved while making their way to the trading posts. These were serious problems, and, besides, they had no need for the goods Henday described. The buffalo provided all they could ever want, and their bows and arrows were all they required to obtain their prey.

Duncan McGillivray, a clerk for the North West Company who recorded this scene, went on to explain the reaction to the proposal:

> The inhabitants of the Plains are so advantageously situated that they could live very happily independent of our assistance. They are surrounded with innumerable herds of various kinds of animals, whose flesh affords them excellent nourishment and whose skins defend them from the inclemency of the weather, and they have invented so many means for the destruction of animals that they stand in no need of ammunition to provide a sufficiency for their purposes. It is then our luxuries that attract them to the fort and make us so necessary to their happiness.

— Excerpted from McGillivray, "Journal," lxix

tribes. The era of the fur trade effectively came to an end around 1840, when men's hats made from far-less-costly silk came on the market.

Treaties and Agreements with the United States

A half century after the Lewis and Clark Expedition, the U.S. government had a plan for establishing the intercontinental network envisioned

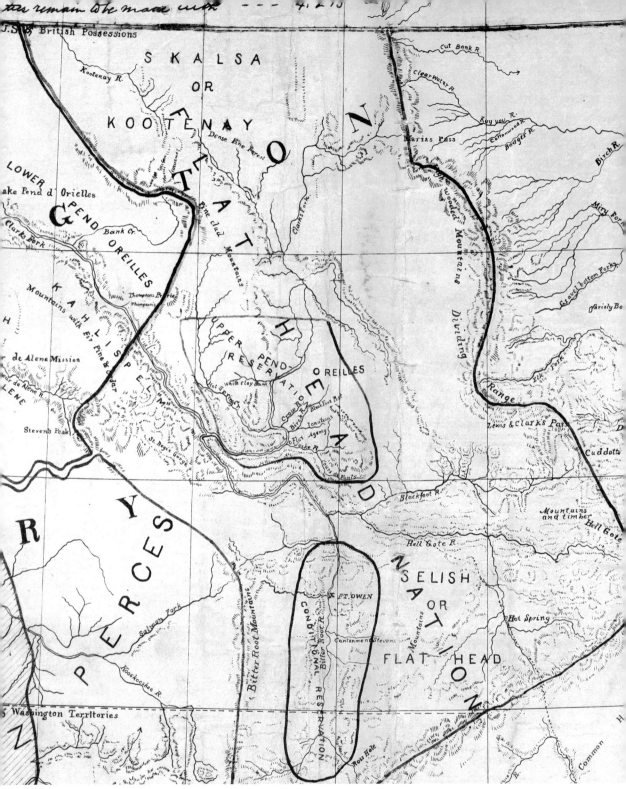

This detail of Isaac I. Stevens's 1857 map shows the results of the 1855 treaty negotiations. The Kootenai tribe's area is marked on the north end of the expanse marked Flathead Nation. Glacier National Park is to the right.   MSCUA, University of Washington Libraries

by Thomas Jefferson. Coast-to-coast commerce required agreements to be negotiated to allow safe passage through Native homelands. Led by Isaac I. Stevens, the Pacific Railway Survey of 1853–1854 proceeded in tandem with negotiating the first treaties affecting the lands now within Glacier National Park.

Kootenai Treaties

Through the ratification of the Hell Gate Treaty, the Kootenais and their neighbors, the Pend d'Oreille and Salish, ceded a vast area of their traditional homelands. Negotiating with Indian Commissioner Isaac Stevens in 1855, the Kootenais and their allies reserved their rights to continue to hunt, fish, and gather in "usual and accustomed" places. These places included the mountains of their traditional territories and many other special places located in what would become Glacier Park.[3]

Vernon Finley, a Kootenai educator, put into perspective his ancestors' lack of understanding about the land cession:

> The idea of owning the land was a foreign concept to traditional Kootenai. Humans were the last to be created and have none of the spiritual power that is contained in the rest of nature. So the idea that humans (whose life span is generally less than one hundred years) could "own" something that was here long before humans existed and will be here long after humans are gone was not previously considered. But from the Western perspective, owning the land is everything. The United States Constitution is based on individual property ownership and protecting those rights. The priority for Isaac Stevens was to secure land from the tribes for settlers wanting to expand into western territory. So the idea of property ownership was one of the largest misunderstandings between the two worldviews.[4]

It took several decades before the lifeways of the Kootenais were seriously affected by the stipulations of the 1855 Treaty of Hell Gate. Until the 1880s, the people continued to live much as they always had, off the bounty of the land. Kootenais remained at the north end of Flathead Lake and in the Tobacco Plains, where they continued to cross the mountains for buffalo as long as there were buffalo to hunt.

After 1880, when buffalo could no longer be found and non-Indian settlements grew around what are now Kalispell and Somers on the

Chief Michelle's Thoughts on the Hell Gate Treaty

▶ ▶ ▶ ▶ ▶ ▶ ▶ ◈ ◀ ◀ ◀ ◀ ◀ ◀ ◀

VERNON Finley, a Kootenai educator, mused on what must have gone through the mind of Chief Michelle in 1855 at the Hell Gate during the negotiations with Governor Isaac Stevens.

> So when Governor Stevens told the Kootenais, "You have to give up ownership of all your aboriginal territories in order to maintain peace with the whites, and we can then reserve a smaller part of what you own and will call it the reservation," the idea was strange to their chief, Michelle. And so what he said was, "Okay, you can say that you own all of this if we can always go where we've always gone to collect the foods and medicines we've always collected and to do the things we've always done in the past." You know, he was trying to figure out a way for both to have their needs met. The chief thought, "You can go ahead and say you own the land, but this earth has been here for thousands of generations, and in a few short years, you're not even going to exist, so the idea that you would own a piece of it is absurd. But if you want to say you own it, go ahead and say you own it as long as we can do what we want to do. And as long as those things are in agreement and you stop killing us, then this can work." So that was his concern with the treaty negotiations.

> —Vernon Finley video-recorded interview

northwest shore of Flathead Lake, the Kootenai settlement at Somers was abandoned. The people joined relatives to the south, along the shores of Big Arm Bay, within the boundaries of the Flathead Indian Reservation that had been created by the 1855 treaty. Eventually, with growing conflicts between non-Indian settlers and the tribes, they were required to have a pass to leave the reservation to hunt or visit their relatives to the north. The massacre of a Pend d'Oreille hunting group in the Swan Valley in 1908 by a game warden made it clear to the people that there were dangers attached to leaving the reservation.[5]

The Ktunaxa in Canada, who lived close to the North Fork of the Flathead, continued to access the western edge of Glacier Park for hunting and trapping well into the early twentieth century, but farther south in Montana, the Ksanka Band was less able to continue these traditional practices outside of the reservation because of state Fish and Game Department laws and growing population pressures.

Blackfeet Treaties

For the Blackfeet, the 1855 Lame Bull, or Judith River, Treaty with the U.S. government guaranteed them a continuing claim to a vast area of their homeland in northern Montana, including the east side of the Rockies from the International Boundary at the forty-ninth parallel south to a line parallel with the headwaters of the Musselshell River. This treaty is remembered by the Blackfeet as Lame Bull's Treaty because he was the first chief to sign.[6]

For concessions granted at the 1855 treaty council, the United States agreed to spend twenty thousand dollars annually for a period of ten years on useful goods and provisions for the tribes of the Blackfeet Nation. This symbol represented 1855 on a winter count, the first year the amount was paid. Paul M. Raczka, *Winter Count: A History of the Blackfoot People* (Brocket, Alta.: Oldman River Cultural Centre, 1979), 53

After the Lame Bull Treaty went into effect, life continued on for the Blackfeet much as it always had. One notable difference was the addition of an Indian agent from the federal government, based at Fort Benton, who was assigned to distribute annuities promised by the treaty. But the annuities were not always sent, and after years of trade in robes, the availability of buffalo, a mainstay commodity, became less and less predictable.

As the Montana gold rush boomed in 1862, the traditional Blackfeet world began to fall apart. Within a few short years, more than fifteen thousand miners were working and exploring in and around Blackfeet country, primarily to the south, in the heart of the treaty-defined shared hunting ground. Some traditional hunting grounds were overrun by miners, and European diseases continued to rage through the camps during these decades. The consequence was that people starved.

Unratified treaties and presidential executive orders between 1865 and 1886 resulted in the loss of millions of acres for the Blackfeet, including

This 1861 winter count symbol for "when they eat dogs" recounts a year of starvation when annuities were not received. Paul M. Raczka, *Winter Count: A History of the Blackfoot People* (Brocket, Alta.: Oldman River Cultural Centre, 1979), 55

key hunting lands and places of spiritual sustenance such as the Sun River country and the Sweet Grass Hills. Intertribal conflicts, hunting pressures, and disease challenged the people's survival, and they sold land for food.[7]

The winter of 1869–1870 was particularly harsh. Some two thousand Blackfeet died of smallpox that winter. On a January morning in 1870, one of the most peaceful bands of the Blackfeet, the Small Robes, suffered a great loss at the hands of the U.S. military. In the military's retaliation for the killing of a white man, 173 people in Chief Heavy Runner's camp— many of whom were women and children—were killed when U.S. troops attacked on that cold winter day. But the Small Robes were innocent. The young men responsible for the killing of the white man were from another band; they had killed in retaliation for the rape of a Pikunni woman. The U.S. military did not verify who was responsible. The memory of the massacre remains etched in Blackfeet history.

In 1882, south of the Sweet Grass Hills, the last Blackfeet buffalo hunt took place. After that hunt, the Blackfeet became completely dependent on government annuities for their survival. Thousands of hungry people moved to the agency on Badger Creek, yet because of unscrupulous agents and an unreliable system, rations were rarely, if ever, available. Again, starvation came down upon the people, this time worse than ever. The winter that followed is still known among the people as Starvation Winter, when hundreds of Pikunni died. Today, the ridge behind Old Agency is called Ghost Ridge because so many people were buried there that year.

Three decades after the Lame Bull Treaty, only a fifth of the original numbers of the Pikunni people remained, and the buffalo were gone. In 1891, just when it seemed things could not get much worse, the Great Northern Railway cut through the heart of the Blackfeet Reservation, setting the stage for land cessions and the creation of Flathead Forest Reserve—and later, Glacier National Park. In 1895, under significant pressure from U.S. government negotiators, including naturalist George Bird Grinnell, the Blackfeet ceded eight hundred thousand acres of mountain lands along the western edge of the Blackfeet Reservation.[8]

For the Blackfeet, this ceded land along the "Backbone of the World" was akin to their church. The mountains held gifts from the Creator, providing for their long-term health and well-being. The high peaks allowed seekers to reach toward Creator Sun while staying connected to Mother Earth. White Calf, the Pikunni chief, complained to the treaty commissioners about the loss of these mountain lands—to no avail.

White Calf's Lament

IN testifying before the U.S. Senate in 1895, White Calf, a Pikunni chief, spoke his mind:

> Chief Mountain is my head. Now my head is cut off. The mountains have been my last refuge. We have been driven here and now we are settled. From Birch Creek to the boundary is what I now give you. I want the timber because in the future my children will need it. . . . The right to hunt . . . the grazing land . . . to fish in the mountains . . . we will sell you the mountain portion of our land. . . . We don't want our Great Father to ask for anything more. We will have to send you away. We don't want our lands allotted. . . . There are many little children going to school and getting an education; there is no end to civilizing our children. They are the ones that will get the benefits from these lands.
>
> —White Calf, testimony before the U.S. Senate

White Calf, Blackfeet chief Montana Historical Society, Helena, 956-020

After the Great Northern Railway cut through the Blackfeet Reservation and the tribe ceded a strip of land on the west side, miners arrived. Above, on the left side, is the boomtown of Altyn located in what is now the Swiftcurrent Valley. T. W. Stanton, photographer, U.S. Geological Survey

In the spring of 1898, soon after the Ceded Strip Agreement took effect, three hundred miners flooded into Blackfeet country, creating the boomtowns of Altyn and St. Mary in the heart of fall hunting territory. Although the Blackfeet had retained rights to hunt and gather in the area, with all these new settlements emerging, along with the general hostility felt toward the tribe, their ability to access the mountains became increasingly more difficult.

Then, with the establishment of Glacier National Park in 1910, the courts ruled that the rights of access to gather and hunt were now extinct. The Blackfeet have never accepted this decision, one that abrogated their 1855 treaty rights in the area as well as the 1895 agreement.

Chapter 4

◈

Knowing the Land

by Sally Thompson

Indigenous place names tell the stories that weave an oral history together. When the stories remain on the land, the people who carry the stories remain in relationship with all that has gone before, and the place remains alive. "Your name is what carries you," explains Vernon Finley, Kootenai language specialist.[1] In the depth of time, every place has a name that holds a cultural memory. In Glacier National Park, these original place names hold a deep and rich history.

Yet, notice the place names on contemporary maps of the park and throughout the area. Most of these names were imposed by Euro-Americans, replacing the original names given by the indigenous groups. Various researchers have tried to document the original place names, with varying degrees of success and with very different results on the east versus the west side of the park.[2]

Visit the east side of Glacier and you are surrounded by peaks with Blackfeet names like Lone Walker and Little Chief. Unfortunately, most of these are not original names but rather replacement names applied by James Willard Schultz in the 1880s in honor of nineteenth-century Blackfeet leaders and friends. Such names include Apikunni, named for Schultz himself, and Grinnell Peak, named for George Bird Grinnell, the naturalist who sometimes traveled with Schultz. Schultz tells of working with two Blackfeet men, Takes-Gun-First and Curly Bear, to erase white

James Willard Schultz and Blackfeet friends at Waterton Lakes, 1931. From left are Far-off White Robe, Otter Woman, Badger Woman, Schultz, Wolf Head, and Weasel Tail. Schultz Collection, Merrill G. Burlingame Special Collections, Montana State University Libraries, Bozeman, 206

names from east-side features "with the exception of the names of the white men who were, or had been, members of the Blackfeet tribes, or who had been closely identified with them as their true friends." Unfortunately, Schultz failed to record most of the original place names while he went about naming mountains for famous Blackfeet leaders and "their true friends," so these names and the knowledge they held are gone.[3]

Place names for the west side, in contrast, were generally left intact until early Glacier Park officials took the initiative to apply new names to much of the landscape. Fortunately, Schultz did not limit his place names research to the Blackfeet. Instead, he recorded traditional Kootenai names as told him by a group of elders at Fort McLeod in the 1920s. One of them was "a half-Kootenai half-Piegan man of great intelligence, named by his Piegan mother, Kakitos' (Star), who gladly acted" as Schultz's interpreter. When Kakitos' told his companions the object of Schultz's visit, "they became quite excited over the opportunity we offered to restore to the west side of Glacier Park the names that their ancestors had given to its various features." Daily sessions went on for a week, during which time Schultz recorded 153 Kootenai place names "with utmost care for accuracy, until we had them all, from the International Boundary south to the southern line of the Park." Most of these names are for landscape features on the west side of the park, although a significant number are located on the east side, documenting the complex history of co-occupancy of this area.[4]

James Willard Schultz with Tobacco Plains Kootenai men, 1930. From left are Schultz, Wolf Going Out of Sight, Jack Ignatius (interpreter), Many Wolves, Water Bull, and Chief Red Horn (Paul David). Schultz Collection, Merrill G. Burlingame Special Collections, Montana State University Libraries, Bozeman, 280

Schultz's biased opinion about Kootenai place names is evident in his comparison of their names to those found in Blackfeet-dominated territory: "Unlike the Blackfeet Tribe's names . . . there is little of romantic interest attached to these Kutenai, west side names," he wrote, "with the exception of the names of various glaciers. They are, for the most part, simply the names of men of the tribe who were successful hunters, or magicians. The Kutenai were not warriors, their coups were the killings of grizzly bears. They were a timid people, passing their lives in the remote fastnesses of the mountains."[5]

From this oversimplification and biased perception—the Kootenais' own description of their seasonal rounds (chapter 5) belies this—it is clear that Schultz understood little about the Kootenais and their lifeways.

Despite this limitation, his efforts have preserved scores of names that might have been lost during the half century that elapsed before another researcher took interest in these place names.[6]

Many place names were missed by researchers, who tended to inquire of tribal elders about names for particular features of the landscape and failed to ask about names for places of cultural importance. The Blackfeet, in particular, given their close proximity, have names for many culturally significant places within the park that were never recorded. One example of this type of place is a favorite berry-picking locale known as "Grey Mare's Tail" in the Two Medicine area.[7]

The purpose here is not to include an exhaustive list of place names but, rather, to acquaint you with the types of names given by the two tribes and to share some stories that will bring the landscape to life.

Kootenai Place Names

Recorded Kootenai place names are concentrated in, but not limited to, the west side of Glacier. The North Fork landscape, in particular, remains rich in Kootenai names, or translations of their names. Get out a map and read the names along Trail Creek, just outside the northwest corner of the park. Add names like Yakinikak and Tuchuck to the more familiar Kintla and Kishenehn inside the park, and you've entered a world before paved roads and engineered trails changed the landscape.

Kootenai place names could come from an event that happened at that site, from a distinctive quality about the site itself, or from a legend tied to that site. These names of places in Glacier can be organized into at least five categories.[8]

Mythic references are found in names such as "Where There's a Big Beaver" (Logging Lake), which comes from a story that tells of a beaver twenty feet long found there, while "Big Belly Man" (Dutch Creek) comes from the paunchy giant who made a trail through this area and who was so huge that he did not feel the sting of arrows. "Red Medicine" (Red Medicine Bow Peak) was so called by the people for the giant who once found a long bow with spiritual energy, either on this peak or on Harris Glacier. Specific details are sometimes lost in the mists of time, but the names prevail. A cluster of glaciers in the park refers to Coyote, the mythical teacher and trickster, and his family. These include "Coyote's Daughter" and "Old Man's Daughter" (Harrison Glacier); "Daughter's Ice" and "No Bear Ice" (Pumpelly Glacier); "Old Woman Ice" (Red Eagle Glacier); and

Logging Lake, shown frozen in this view, was known in the Kootenai language as "Where There's a Big Beaver" Lake. Glacier National Park, 1276

"Coyote's Son Ice" and "Wild Rhubarb Blossom Ice" (Sperry Glacier). Coyote had a son, Rhubarb, whom he tried to entertain by sliding down the ice. But the plan turned tragic, for while Coyote played, his little boy grew colder and colder and finally froze to death.

Plant references are found in the many places in the North Fork region of the park that are named for plants found in the area, including "Place of Red Willows" (Akokala Creek and Lake); "Big Strawberries" (Bowman Creek); "Head of Rhubarb Lake" (Upper Quartz Lake); "Where the Rhubarb Is Long" (Lower Quartz Lake); "Small Camas Lake" (Arrow Lake); and Camas Creek. A question that comes up in relation to Rhubarb is whether these names refer to places where wild rhubarb can be found or to Coyote's son, Wild Rhubarb. When Vernon Finley was asked whether the plant or the mythical being was the correct interpretation, he laughed and replied, "It might be both and more."[9]

References to people include place names that are based on tribal leaders, for example, "Weasel Collar" (Carter Glacier and Mountain); "Black Bear Hat" (Cerulean Mountain); "Chief Coming Back" (Gardner Point

Mountain); "Chased in the Woods" (Mount Geduhn); "Wolf Gun" (Loneman Mountain); and "Sacred Rock" (Debris Mountain).

References to cultural activities or observations include names such as "Dead Man's Creek" (Starvation Creek); "Lost Rider " (Howe Lake); "Traders Lake" (Roger's Lake); "A Good Place to Dance" (Apgar area); and "Ice Where the Goats' Children Play" (Baby Glacier). Schultz was told that "in former days, the Kutenai Indians slid down this glacier at the time they were having their annual religious ceremony at Sacred Dancing Lake."[10] On the east side of the Continental Divide, you'll find "Standing Lodge Pole of a Medicine Lodge" (Lee Creek); "Where Rawhide Was Stretched Across the River to Pull Tipi Bundles Across" (St. Mary River); and "Jealous Woman" (Swiftcurrent Lake). This original Kootenai name for Swiftcurrent Lake (previously known as Lake McDermott) comes from a Kootenai story about two sisters married to the same man.

Swiftcurrent Lake, known by the Kootenais as "Jealous Woman Lake" T. J. Hileman, photographer, Glacier National Park, 1276

How Jealous Woman Lake Got Its Name

LONG ago, a good and brave Kootenai hunter married twin sisters. These sisters were identical except that one, named Camas, talked slowly, the other, named Marmot, talked very, very fast. Marmot was jealous of Camas and complained to their husband. Camas told her sister that she had nothing to be jealous of, that their husband loved them both and that she loved her twin sister as well. But Marmot couldn't trust the situation and believed she was neglected. More and more she complained. Their husband told her he loved them equally.

The husband took his bow and arrows to the edge of the lake, where he heard splashing and saw two otters playing. He shot one and then tried to get the other, but couldn't. He was sorry because he wanted each of his wives to have one of these medicine skins. He took the one home and gave it to Camas, telling Marmot he would bring her the other the next day. But he wasn't able. For many days he searched along the river but was unable to spot another otter.

Marmot grew angrier and angrier that her sister had an otter skin and she did not. She said to her sister: "I have proof now that our man loves you best. He gave you the otter; he does not even try to get one for me. He hunts other animals every day, bighorn, goats, animals that live nowhere near the haunts of the otter."

Camas argued that he had tried and tried to get her an otter skin but that he had to keep them supplied with meat; "that is why he hunts the mountain animals." But, no matter what Camas said, Marmot would not believe that her husband loved her as much as Camas. Marmot told her sister she hated her and that they couldn't continue to both live as wives to the same man. She challenged to fight in any way that Camas chose, to determine which one would stay with the husband.

Camas replied that they had no weapons but that they could swim across the lake and back, over and over, until one of them is too tired to continue, and drowns. "Now, crazy woman," she said to her sister, "what do you say to that?" Marmot didn't waste any time, but ran to the water and the two began "their swim of hate."

They crossed the lake; turned and came back; crossed again and started back, Camas well in the lead. She reached the shore in front of the lodge, dragged herself out on the shore, and turned. Her sister had gone down. There was not even a ripple on the still water. Marmot was drowned.

When the husband returned from hunting, he found Camas crying in the lodge. When she told him what had happened, he cried too. They looked, but were unable to find the body of the lost one. So they moved away from the unhappy place and returned to the camp of their people, but it was a long time, a very long time, before they ceased mourning, and never again would they go anywhere near the lake.

"Yes, this is the Lake of the Jealous Woman!"

—Adapted from Schultz, *Blackfeet Tales of Glacier National Park*, 229–322

References to landscape features are easily found in names such as "Sitting Porcupine" (Square Peak); "Standing Arrow" (Pumpelly Pillar); "Green-Blue Ridge" (Parke Ridge); "Broad Body" (Pocket Lake); "The Long Lake" (Upper Waterton Lake); and "Where a Person Is Brought Back to Where He Started" (McDonald Creek between Lake McDonald and Logan Creek).

The meaning of some place names has escaped understanding, such as "Ear Fastened to Skin," which today is known as Snyder Ridge. Over time, some names survive without clear attribution. One of the most interesting of these is "Hand Mountain." As the story goes, White Raven, an 'Aqłsmaknik, obtained his name and power from the peak with the same name (White Crow Mountain) that lies west of Chief Mountain. Close by is a place called "Hand Mountain" by the Kootenais, the exact location of which is unknown. Some believe this mountain is the one now known as Citadel Peaks.[11] Ambrose Gravelle, an elder from the Tobacco Plains Band, long ago told Claude Schaeffer that it consisted of five peaks called "Hands of the Mountains . . . east of Kintla between the headwaters of Waterton and Flathead drainages." The name might have come from the five peaks looking like the fingers of a hand, or because travelers had to scale the peaks, hand over hand. People who climbed all five peaks for visions would be rewarded with great power. The Kootenais traveled to this area in all seasons, but took different trails, depending on their mode of transportation. On horseback they would take a trail that circled around the Hand; on snowshoes they climbed over the divide between the thumb and the forefinger.[12]

In 2009, at a gathering of Kootenai elders held at the Flathead Lake Biological Station, Jon Mahseelah spoke of an important power place near the Glacier-Waterton boundary where there is a deep hole. Claude Schaeffer had been told a similar story nearly a century earlier. According to Mahseelah, people used to go there and circle the hole three times before climbing down into it to gain the power to become a medicine man. The same general area was also known for a mysteriously loud booming sound. Kootenai elders' description of the noise is reminiscent of the booming sound heard by Meriwether Lewis while he was exploring the Sun River country, southeast of Glacier, in 1805. This booming phenomenon remains a source of speculation.[13]

Few original Kootenai words remain on the map of Glacier Park. Kintla means "sack." The upper lake is called Kintla Nana Akuqnuk, meaning "little gunny sack." It is said that Indians usually avoided the

Pumpelly Pillar was known as "Standing Arrow" to the Kootenais. T. J. Hileman, photographer, Glacier National Park, 1033

waters of Kintla and that when one of them drowned there, the body was never recovered. Kishenehn is the name of a creek paralleled by an ancient Kootenai trail in the northwestern corner of the park. The trail followed the creek from the North Fork of the Flathead River to the Akamina Road that drops into the Waterton area. Although Jack Holterman reports that the name translates to mean either "no good" or "white fir" (balsam), contemporary Kootenai speakers don't recognize this word or even its sounds—for example, there is no "sh" sound in Kootenai. This place name is associated with a legend about a Pikunni boy whom the Kootenais had adopted. According to the legend, when this boy, Kishenehn, grew up, he returned to his own people across the mountains. Some Kootenais were angry at him and followed him, intending to do him harm. Heading toward Akamina Pass, they ran into Kishenehn along the creek that now bears his name and shot him with their arrows. He had special powers that protected him, so he only laughed as their arrows bounced off him. He laughed too soon, however. The arrow of Unknown Bear finally pierced and killed Kishenehn.[14]

Blackfeet Place Names

The vast majority of Blackfeet names are located on the east side of the Continental Divide. As mentioned, most of the names that appear to be Blackfeet were not the original names but ones conferred by James Willard Schultz. Original Blackfeet place names translated into English include familiar names such as Chief Mountain, Belly River, Cutbank Creek, Flattop Mountain, and Swiftcurrent Creek.

Blackfeet names for features within Glacier Park, like Kootenai names, can be organized into five categories.[15]

Descriptive names include Chief Mountain, which stands out ahead of the other peaks; "The Needles" (Citadel Mountain); Cutbank Creek; "On Top Prairie" (Flattop Mountain); "Wide Forest" (Hudson Bay Divide); "Spotted Ice" (Ahern Glacier); "Red Mountain" (Rising Wolf); "Bear Mountain" (Marias Pass); and "Lakes Inside" (St. Mary Lakes).

Mythic names attach to several places around what is now Singleshot Mountain, which was originally called Old Man by the Blackfeet. (Napi's Point remains today as a reminder of that earlier name for the mountain.) The Creator put Old Man, or Napi, here as a "little male helper," and Napi provided everything for the Blackfeet. Napi's Point stands at the north end of Flattop Mountain and remains an important place to the people

"Old Man" in the Blackfeet language (now Singleshot Mountain) and Napi's Point (the sharp peak on the right) Glacier National Park, 4495

around the community of Babb, the northernmost settlement on the Blackfeet Reservation. One name for Rising Wolf is Holy Woman Rock, a place where women went to find their medicine.[16]

Plant names are limited within the park today to only one site. Baring Creek carries the name "Weasel Eyes," which in Blackfeet refers to huckleberries. You might have enjoyed these berries after the long hike over Siyeh Pass, on the way down to Sunrift Gorge. Sikokini Springs is another Blackfeet name that refers to a plant, the birch, but it is located outside the park to the southwest.

Animal names attach to a number of places that carry the original Blackfeet names for animals, such as "Breaks the Tail," or "Mule Deer" (Boulder Creek and Ridge); Otter Lake (Elizabeth Lake); "Where There Are a Lot of Goats" (Goat Haunt); Mink Creek (Wilbur Creek); Fox Creek; and Elk Creek.

Cultural observations once informed Blackfeet names for specific sites, including "Where the Bigfoot [Caribou] Was Killed" (Hanging Gardens); "Where the Warriors Go Up" (Ahern Pass); "Where We Fought the

Square-topped Chief Mountain from Lee Creek, looking west, 1939 I. B. Solberg, photographer, Glacier National Park, HPF 4622

The Origin of Two Medicine Lake

THE buffalo no longer wandered the prairie, and the grass was wilted and brown. The streams no longer ran full and deep. In the glare of the sun, the parched earth lay burning, for drought had come into the country of the Blackfoot, and with the drought came famine. Many miles wandered the hunters in search of game, only to return empty-handed and with waning strength. Bad days had come to the Blackfoot nation, and powerful ceremonies were to be held in the hope of securing relief.

Along the shore of a well-loved lake, two medicine lodges had been built, and here the ceremonies were carried on. Chants were sung and heard by Old Man. Through His spirit helpers, He sent word to the suffering nation that they must send seven of their oldest and wisest men to the top of the mountain [Chief Mountain] where the Wind Spirit lived. It was the Wind Spirit who was causing the drought, and it was he who must be appeased.

And so the seven were selected and sent forth to climb the steep mountain to its summit. But when they reached the top, the Wind Spirit was such an awe-inspiring person that their hearts failed them and they turned and fled in fear. Therefore the drought continued, the suffering increased, and the Blackfoot were in desperate straits.

Now Old Man sent word again, this time that fourteen of the young warriors must journey to the home of the Wind Spirit. The fourteen bravest were selected—those who had earned many of the hard-won eagle plumes and whose deeds were most often recounted about the evening camp fires. They made their way up the trail until they, too, stood upon the mountain crest.

The Wind Spirit waited in the door of his lodge, dreadful to behold. But these were warriors, tried and true, and though they were fearful they were brave as well. They gave no sign of weakness but drew nearer until they could reach out and touch the robe of this Mighty One. Their courage pleased the Wind Spirit greatly. He sent them home with these words to carry to their people. "Now am I sure that the Blackfoot are a nation of men and deserving of my favor." He brought forth the life-giving rains and poured them down upon the parched land, drenching the earth with the cool, sweet water.

When the young men reached the lake shore, they found the grass growing thick and green, the streams replenished, and the buffalo returned. From that day forth there was happiness and prosperity where dwelt the bands of the Blackfoot nation.

—Gridley, *Indian Legends,* 73–74

Two Medicine Lake T. J. Hileman, photographer, Glacier National Park, 1107

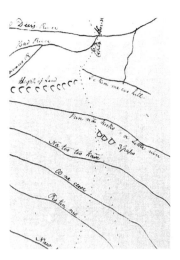

Detail of an 1801 map with Blackfeet place names provided to Peter Fidler by Akomakki. It shows Na too too kase—"Place of Two Medicine Lodges"—now known as the Two Medicine River. Hudson's Bay Company Archives, Archives of Manitoba, Peter Fidler fonds, Sketch map "Drawn by the Feathers or ac ko mok ki a Black foot chief 7th Feby 1801," HBCA E.3/2 fos, 106d-107

Kootenais" (Waterton Valley, just north of Kootenai Pass); "The Mountain Where Someone Froze" (Kootenai Peak); "Rope Across" or "Rope Stretched" (Lee Creek); "Bull Pound River" and "River of Many Chiefs Gathering" (St. Mary River, below the lakes); and "Old Trail Passing by the Mountains" (Old North Trail).

Where ancient Blackfeet names remain on the landscape, so do their stories. Many Napi stories take place in the mountains, including creation stories. For instance, Napi took a piece of Chief Mountain to create the Sweet Grass Hills. Percy Bullchild, a Pikunni, shares an important story about one of the first people, Crowfeather Arrow, who hid the buffalo in a place now within Glacier Park. Jealous, vengeful, and desirous of power, Crowfeather Arrow decided to hide all the buffalo so the people wouldn't find them. Using the supernatural power entrusted to him by Creator Sun, he rounded up all of the buffalo and hid them in a mountain canyon at the head of present-day Cutbank Creek. Fortunately for the people, clever and generous Bellyfat was able to outsmart Crowfeather Arrow and free the buffalo so the people wouldn't starve.[17]

Working with Akomakki, a Siksika leader in 1801, Peter Fidler recorded names of many rivers along the east side of the mountains. One of these, matching the location of the Two Medicine River today, is listed as Na too too kase, which means "Place of Two Medicine Lodges."[18]

Moving through the Landscape

Many of the same trails and roads used by visitors in the park today are those that the tribes of the area have used since time immemorial, making them a fascinating way to reimagine the landscape. Indian trails are often thought of as narrow passages through the woods, much like deer trails—and some of them were. Others were substantial. When William Clark traveled overland in July 1805 along the Missouri River south of the Great Falls, he "passed over a mountain on an Indian rode by which rout I cut off Several miles of the Meanderings of the River, the roade which passes this mountian is wide and appears to have been dug in maney places."[19] His party was traveling along what is now known as the Old North Trail.

Some of the trails across Glacier were also more like roads, cleared of trees to make room for hundreds of people and even more horses. In 1896, Walter McClintock, accompanied by a Blackfeet guide, traveled from the west side of what is now Glacier Park over Cutbank Pass along a trail "worn deep into the ground by generations of Blackfeet and other Indian tribes, when they crossed and re-crossed the Rocky Mountains on their war and hunting expeditions."[20]

Cutbank Pass and Dry Fork Valley looking east Glacier National Park, 1873

Historically, Glacier's trails were used by both the Kootenais and the Blackfeet for various purposes—to gather food, to trade and visit, sometimes to steal horses, and at other times to wage battle. But the trails were most commonly used as part of the food-gathering cycle. Some trails were better ascended from one direction than the other, and some could be used during one season but not another. Some were used predominantly by the Kootenais and others predominantly by the Blackfeet. Some were well suited to pedestrian travel but not appropriate for horses. There were some that admitted the use of a travois, although not many in these mountains.

Traveling with a Travois

NICHOLAS Point, a Jesuit priest who traveled much of this vast landscape in the 1840s, described the details of travel with a travois—"a kind of vehicle without wheels"—behind a horse, pointing out that the mountain Indians did not regularly use the travois since the narrow trails and steep ascents made it difficult to keep the travois upright. According to Father Point:

> On the narrow roads or paths the contrivance would be altogether useless. As for the steep ascents, the use of the travois on them would be very difficult. Even on the most gentle slopes the woman leading the horse has to pull and the man has to push from behind. If this help is not given, the whole load may slide back and sometimes be strewn about, especially when the terrain on which they are traveling slopes just as much sidewise as it does lengthwise. I once saw a horse stop on an almost perpendicular slope on a little rock promontory from which it could move only by making a leap of more than fifty feet. The owner of the horse had no choice other than to lose his horse or make it jump. One does not always come off so easily. In place of a single horse, think of an entire equipage, and, and in addition to this, children or infirm people. Then you will understand why this means of travel is used only on the plains. Sometimes a dog may take the place of the horse. But the load and the size of the vehicle must be proportionate to the strength of the poor beast.
>
> —Point, *Wilderness Kingdom*, 205

Blackfeet horse travois American Museum of Natural History, 31646

45

Trail through The Big Gap, as known to the Kootenais (now Marias Pass) Yale Collection of Western Americana, Beinecke Rare Book and Manuscript Library, New Haven, Connecticut, 1116462

From the time that the great ice sheets of the Late Pleistocene receded, travelers had to contend with the dictates of these mountains. Following the lead of the four-legged creatures, the people learned the best routes of travel over passes. The early residents of the area knew the landscape thoroughly and traveled everywhere that a path could be followed. Many of the drainages of the North Fork of the Flathead, such as Quartz Creek, had trails and were used for hunting deer and elk, fishing, and plant gathering but were too steep and rough to be used in crossing the Continental Divide.[21]

Major expeditions across the mountains had to be funneled through eleven passes, from South Kootenay Pass in Waterton Lakes National Park to the southern boundary of Glacier at Marias Pass. Stories of some of these passes help us imagine the challenges of travel in the days before the park.

Traveling options were influenced by a number of factors, including seasonal characteristics. High water in late spring made some trails too "boggy" for people and horses, although these same routes might be preferred when the cold winds of autumn started to blow. Gentle slopes were sought for crossing winter snowfields, away from steep slopes that might be the source of an avalanche. Travelers needed to understand subtle details of the weather such as the amount of moisture in snow, the character of the clouds, and the nature of the wind.

Food requirements also influenced travel choices. Tobacco Plains elder Ambrose Gravelle recalled that "the band or bands would split up and the smaller groups would take separate trails eastward, so as to have access to more game on the journey."[22]

Marias Pass, or "The Big Gap," as it was known by the Kootenais, is familiar to park visitors along U.S. Highway 2. This route was favored by the Ksanka Band for spring and fall buffalo hunting trips because it was an easier trail for horses than the Middle Fork trails to the south. The pass was not used by the Kootenais from the 1830s to the 1860s, perhaps because of a belief that "it was stopped" by evil spirits. In the 1860s, Kootenai chief Aeneas and his party, traveling in the winter on snowshoes, attempted to clear the trail of debris that had accumulated from the long

Aeneas Paul, Kootenai chief Glacier National Park, HPF 4887

period without use. Despite their work, with so many years of disuse, the trail remained rough and accessible only during times of low water. After this time, the Kootenais referred to the route as the Aeneas Trail.[23]

From the Blackfeet side on the east, Marias Pass is known as "The Backbone." Hugh Monroe told Schultz about his first trip up that pass with Red Crow in the 1830s. As they ascended the South Fork of Two Medicine River to the pass, Red Crow pointed out "a high, sharp-peaked mountain on the north side of the gap" and told Monroe that the Pikunni called it Makikinsi Istuki, or "Backbone Mountain." When asked about this trail of three or four deep-worn, parallel paths, Red Crow explained that it was "a good one not a dangerous place in its whole length across to the Big Lake of the Kal-i-spels. It is much used by all of the West-Side tribes, sneaking across to kill our buffalo when they are sure that we are encamped far out on the plains. Yes, and our war parties often follow it when they go upon West-Side raids."[24]

By the 1850s, the Marias Pass trail and "a deserted encampment of last summer indicates that this pass is occasionally frequented by the Flatheads or the Kootenaies, for the purpose of hunting elk and deer, which are numerous here." The once well-defined trail had become "no more than a narrow foot-path although the decayed stumps and trunks of trees clearly indicated that a broad road had once been cleared."[25]

Another "well-worn Indian trail" followed Swiftcurrent Creek through what is now another popular area of the park, around the Many Glacier Hotel. George Bird Grinnell, in 1891, witnessed evidence of Kainai hunting camps all over the area: "Once these mountains abounded in sheep and goats, and everywhere about this park may be seen the sites of old Indian camps, with rotting lodge poles, old fireplaces and piles of bone and hair, showing where game has been cut up and hides dressed."[26]

Many trails led into and around the St. Mary area, much as they do today. In 1885, when Schultz and Grinnell were hunting up the west side of the Upper St. Mary Lake, they

> came to an old Kootenai trail, which we were told reached across the range into Missoula. This we followed through dense quaking asp[en] groves, thickets of pine, and down timber, and after about two hours' ride came to a long park pretty well up on the side of the mountain. . . . Riding through this park we came to an immense limestone ledge which reached from the mountain to the water's edge, terminating in a cut bluff. Running up the nearly perpendicular side of this ledge is an old elk trail, and we could see

Looking from Swiftcurrent Pass into Many Glacier Valley T. J. Hileman, photographer, Glacier National Park, 4137

that the Indians had gone over it with their horses, but we thought
it too risky a place for our animals.

The noted mountainside is in the Rising Sun area and is likely the cut
bluff now known as the Golden Stairs.[27]

In the Upper St. Mary Valley, during the summer of 1891, Grinnell and
Schultz saw cut stumps, ten feet tall, that had been cut by the Kootenais
when the snow was that deep, presumably to clear the trail. Approaching
the top of the pass, they were able to follow an old trail by following the
old cuttings of the stunted trees.[28]

Some extremely challenging trails were used because, despite their
difficulty, they led to important resources. The daunting pass that millions
of park visitors know as Logan Pass along the Going-to-the-Sun Road

St. Mary Lake Trail going toward Gunsight Pass on the northwest side of the lake
T. J. Hileman, photographer, Glacier National Park, 3170

was crossed in winter by the Kootenais, who call it "Pull the Packs Up," or, literally, "Where Packs Are Pulled Up on a Line," referencing the steep cliff ledges near the top.

In the 1930s, Chief Paul David of the Tobacco Plains Band told Claude Schaeffer of a winter trip through the mountains in the 1860s, when he was a young man. After preparing snowshoes at a camp located where the town of Columbia Falls is today, a large group of Kootenais, on a mission for the Flathead Reservation Indian agent, traveled along the Flathead River through Bad Rock Canyon, then up to the West Glacier area. From there, they walked across the frozen lake now carrying the name McDonald and followed McDonald Creek to Logan Creek, which they followed up to the pass. The valley between the lake and Logan Creek was known to the Kootenais as "Where a Person Falls Back," or, more simply, Avalanche Creek, which today has the same reputation for danger from snowslides.[29]

Today, as you travel Going-to-the-Sun Road you can see the steep cliff as you parallel Logan Creek and approach the summit of the pass. Imagine fifty or sixty Kootenais—men, women, and children—having just survived a modest avalanche, managing to scale this cliff. Their ingenious method and the skill required to succeed would impress any experienced climber. As Paul David reported:

> Here the men stood on each others shoulders to climb to the different rock shelves. There were seven shelves and a man was stationed on each one, to assist in pulling up the people and equipment. The equipment was pulled to the top first; then the babies in the cradle boards and then the children and women. Two rawhide thongs were used, one of which had a loop in the end which was taken around a person's hand, while he pulled and steadied himself by using the other thong. In this [way] the entire party scaled this rocky wall.[30]

Once on top, they sent their packs sliding down the snow, then slid along behind them to the bottom, where they followed the frozen surface of the creek to St. Mary Lake, on the east side of what is now the park.

Logan Pass in winter Glacier National Park, 1737

Cutbank Pass trail, 1907 Yale Collection of Western Americana, Beinecke Rare Book and Manuscript Library, Yale
University, New Haven, Connecticut, 1090118

This was an important place where buffalo could be found in winter on the south-facing grassy slopes above the lake. The group also hunted bighorns in this same area, with the help of trained dogs. They would run upslope on Red Eagle Mountain to drive sheep down to the frozen surface of the lake.

Some trails were selected because they were less vulnerable to ambush. If ambush was feared, people traveled en masse, relying on the safety of numbers. Trader and government agent William Hamilton, traveling with one companion, stumbled into such a situation in 1858. These white men came upon a group of about forty Kootenai headmen holding a council in the area of St. Mary Lake. They were part of a larger village of about three hundred men and their families. The leaders were discussing the best route to take across the mountains to escape Blackfeet who would soon be retaliating for the death of some of their own at the hands of the Kootenais.[31]

Walter McClintock was told that Cutbank Pass was used by the Blackfeet for making war on the west-side tribes, the Pend d'Oreille, Kootenai, and Salish. The Blackfeet accessed this pass from its gentle approach along Cutbank Creek, where they had a traditional campground in a large meadow near a big fir tree. This location is in the vicinity of the campground available to park visitors today.[32]

The Pikunni remembered a story about Mad Wolf and a war party that were returning on one of these trails from a raid on the Salish when they encountered a group of Kootenais who were returning from east of the mountains. A battle ensued, and only a lone Kootenai woman survived to return home to tell the story.[33]

Since Cutbank Pass was one of the most frequently used trails by the Blackfeet, the Kootenais traveled with great caution when they headed toward the divide. Paul David reported that "the mother of John Star and a number of other Indians [Kutenais] were surprised by the Piegan on Nyack Creek and during the battle Chief Baptiste of the Akiyinik was killed."[34]

Fear of traveling the Cutbank Pass trail was not confined to the Kootenais. In the 1930s, Art Whitney, a forester, "met an elderly Blackfeet lady guiding prospectors; she told him that during her youth her people never went up the Middle Fork of the Flathead as it was too easy for the Kutenai to ambush them in the gorge area." But despite fear of conflict, the trail was commonly used through the 1870s.[35]

Other stories of incidents between Blackfeet and Kootenais have survived, but many more have not. Raids for horses, or for women and children, were common. On one occasion, a group from the Small Robe Band of Pikunni, led by Bear Chief, raided the Kootenais for horses and headed home with sixty or seventy of the animals. The Kootenais followed them back across the divide, only to be chased back, empty-handed, by the Pikunni.[36]

These same trails are accessible to park visitors today. If you've traveled any of these particular routes, you've had the pleasure of knowing the landscape and the landmarks of the area, the vegetation and sheer cliffs, the waterfalls and rockslides. If not, you can simply put your imagination to work. When and if you do travel these trails, try to recall this old way of life, when buffalo still roamed the edges of the mountains and people still planted the sacred tobacco seeds.

Chapter 5

◈

The Kootenai Worldview

BY THE KOOTENAI CULTURE COMMITTEE

Learning from Our Ancestors

THE traditional Kootenai stories both reflect and construct the worldview of the people. Within each of the stories is an awareness of the presence of the spiritual part of everything in the physical world. And everything in the physical world is connected through a giant network. Together they give us an awareness of our place in the world.

According to the Kootenai stories, the earth was first inhabited by spirits placed here by the Creator. The spirits became a part of all the animals, plants, and everything we as humans can perceive. Many of the stories are about incidences of contact between humans and the spirit within a plant, animal, or something else in existence. Our survival here on earth was possible only with the help from the spirits. The spirit would choose a person to contact and teach a song, or songs, in order for the person to attain whatever type of help was being offered by the spirit.

The Kootenai worldview resulted after thousands of generations of communication between spirits and humans. It includes the belief that everything has a spirit and all of creation is connected like a giant web. There are no extra parts, inanimate objects, or coincidences.

The Spirits Speak to the Kootenais

A long time ago, when the Creator first made the earth, he put here the spirits. None of the spirits had any particular physical form. But they each had their own songs. How it was known which spirits were present at any given time and place was from the song that was being sung.

One day the Creator called the spirits all together and told them, "I'm going to put human beings here on the earth and they're going to be naked and helpless. So it will be up to you to decide whether they're going to survive or not. You will have to decide how you will be perceived by humans and whether you're going to help or hinder their survival."

So the spirits stood up, one by one, and said what they would become. For example, one said, "I'll be the buffalo and I'll provide food and shelter." So all of them took their turn and stood up and said how they would be perceived by humans. It was always understood that not all the spirits participated. So we always knew that there was much more to reality than what humans are capable of perceiving. When the spirits all had spoken, the Creator placed human beings on the earth.

But before he made human beings, he told the spirits, "What you'll take with you are your songs as your form of communication. Humans will not have direct communication with me, and it will be through you that they will receive spiritual help." The spirits were to decide which humans they were going to help. They would then let that person learn their song and give that person a small task to perform in order to access their spiritual help. To all the rest of us, we would simply hear whatever noise that spirit's being was making.

So, if I were the right individual and that spirit wanted to come and help me, I would be able to hear the song that it was singing. Like that breeze that just went through here, that wind. The right ones would hear the song that is being sung in that. But they'd hear the song outside of what we perceive with our ears. Like the chirping of the birds, there is a song being sung in that. There's a song being sung in the water, and if we were the right individuals we would hear those songs, and then that spirit would teach us that song and tell us exactly what we had to do in order to access their help. All the rest of us would only hear wind blowing, birds chirping, or water flowing.

Then the Creator made the human beings. Everything that we see, everything that we hear, everything that we touch, everything that we smell, everything we feel, everything that we sense, it was all there as spirit that day and this is what it became.

During that first year that the human beings were here on this earth, they started to wander around in the territory and different spirits would help them out, helping them to survive—giving them food and shelter and everything.

And so everything that we see, everything that we hear has a spirit in it. And that is what shaped our worldview. The ʾAqⱡsmaknik realized that we aren't the dominant force in this universe. We're the youngest brother of all of Creation. And you carry yourself that way in the rest of Creation. We wouldn't be here without the help of everything that's here.

—As told by Vernon Finley, Kootenai educator

The traditional Kootenai elders were aware that we were the last to be created (the youngest brother), with none of the inherent spiritual power possessed by all the other creations. This is in sharp contrast to the Western view, which places man on top of a hierarchy with the rest of creation at our disposal. Much of the history of contact between cultures has been about attempts to westernize the worldview of Native peoples, and so it has been for the Kootenai people. The result has been acculturation in attitude and behaviors, to varying degrees, among the present-day Kootenais.

The traditional seasonal round of the Kootenais was informed all along the way by this communication with spirits. We, as the youngest brother, didn't presume to make choices without help and guidance from the spirits. To understand us requires an understanding of this essential relationship.

The Kootenai lifestyle, before the reservation era, was migratory but far from random. We knew every aspect of our homeland. We knew where to find reliable root crops and berries and where to find potable water and rich fields of grass to sustain our tired horses after a journey across the mountains. We knew what to expect as the seasons unfolded, year after year, and we kept track of where we were as the planet cycled around the sun.

The traditional Kootenai calendar started with midwinter. To keep track, each man provided himself with a length of rawhide rope. When the band agreed that a new year had begun, each would tie a knot in his string, and throughout the year, a new knot was tied at each new moon. They added coloring for specific events, like births, deaths, and special occasions. In this way, we kept account of the months and the seasons.

We would set up camp in the locations of seasonal food resources and follow them up and down the mountains with the changing seasons. During various seasons, the parklands of the high country were considered home. We knew each pathway over the mountains, those that were conducive to pedestrian or horse travel and those better suited to winter travel on snowshoes. We knew areas where we were vulnerable to attack from enemies and created strategies to travel across the landscape as carefully as possible as we moved from one food source to another.

These trips were never single purpose or destination dominated. Think, instead, of full engagement with one's surroundings and with multiple opportunities to acquire food and medicine as needed and generally to enjoy life. Our lifestyle involved hunting various species of animals, including birds and fish, and we carried the tools to be successful in these

ʼA·kiⱡkakukuⱡ, The Four Seasons

LONG ago there used to be twenty-four months in a year.

There were twelve months of winter and twelve months of summer.

When it was winter, it would be a long time before spring.

The spirits whittled a supply of green wood. The wood was put into the fire.

When the green wood was all burned up, then it was spring.

The fire kept burning. It was a long time—twelve months—before it completely burned.

Then, when the seasons changed, when it was winter again,

Then the spirits were very hungry, there was no more food.

They were badly off, the spirits lived pitifully.

Then Coyote approached Squirrel.

She told him: "There is no more food. Now my children and I are very hungry.

My children and I have already eaten all the food that I cached. Now I have nothing to eat.

It has been a very long season. It is much, much too long a winter.

We should do something to shorten the season. It is very bad that the season is so long.

If what they say is true, that the people will multiply,

They will be very pitiful if the winter is twelve months long."

Then Coyote told her: "You should cry. Cry, cry, keep crying.

I will ask, Why does the old woman keep crying?

She has been crying for so long she has given herself a headache.

Then I'll come over and ask you [why are you crying].

You will say that is a very long season (winter), that you are hungry,

That you and your children are hungry."

Then Coyote went back out.

In just a little while, Squirrel began to cry, she cried, and cried, and cried, and cried.

When the people went over and asked, "What is she saying?" she did not listen.

She just cried and cried.

Then Coyote went back there.

"What do you keep saying? You are giving yourself a headache.

Why do you keep crying?"

"Oh, it has been a very long season. My children and I are hungry.

My children and I have already eaten all the berries that I cached.

There is no more here. Now we are very hungry.

It is a very long season, twelve months of winter. We should do something.

It should be spring. The winter is too long."

Coyote went out and informed the whole camp.

"Squirrel said that she and her children are starving because the season is so long

And that the spirits should do something to shorten the season.

Twelve months is much too long a winter."

—As told by Mary Andrew, Kootenai elder

Snowshoe trail Yale Collection of Western Americana, Beinecke Rare Book and Manuscript Library, Yale University, New Haven, Connecticut, 1116538

pursuits. Food restrictions were based on good stewardship of the land, and these rules were not to be broken unless people were starving. If it was a bad year and the group had to move in search of food, those who were unable to travel had to stay behind and eat whatever they could. If you had to break a food rule and take an animal out of season, you prayed to keep yourself spiritually clean.

In addition to tool kits and some dried food, we carried pouches of dried herbal medicines for the various ailments we might encounter.

Although medicinal plants are everywhere, they have to be gathered at the right time of year, then processed and stored for the times when they're needed. Plant knowledge was essential. You had to know which ones were for healing and which ones could poison.

The journey to a new camp location was more than a means to an end. Food and medicine were gathered along the way, important places along the trails were revisited, and laughter was common. Stick games, horse racing, and storytelling contributed to the wealth of daily life. The spirit of all things was acknowledged. The traditional Kootenai lifeway was one of full living in response to the foods that the unfolding seasons provided.

The Kootenai people, before the time of Glacier and Waterton National Parks, lived in a land of familiarity and abundance. Our ancestors knew that if they listened to the spirits as they had been instructed at the beginning of time and lived in accordance with these instructions, life would be good. They understood the relationships among all life, and knew, during rare times of scarcity and famine, that life was out of balance and they had a role in adjusting the balance.

Kootenai winter camp, ca. 1902 Archives and Special Collections, Mansfield Library, University of Montana, Missoula, 82.0226

By the end of the nineteenth century, when our ancestors were confined to reservations, this lifeway slowly came to an end. Without the capacity to travel throughout this vast homeland to gather and hunt the foods that had sustained us since the beginning of time, our people had to adapt to the ways of the Euro-Americans who settled all around us. We have not forgotten, though, what we were taught at the beginning of time. We still listen for what the spirits are trying to tell us, we still eat many of the traditional foods, and the elders still tell of the days when our ancestors crossed what is now Logan Pass on snowshoes in the sparkling light of winter.

For the last century, many elders have told anthropologists and historians of these old ways. We are the true authors of this account. Those who recorded these stories, or learned from the ones who did, are appreciated for what they have helped to preserve.

Around the Seasons

Nakta'suk (January), or "After Chinook, Layers of Ice with Water in Between"

Also known as "Time of the Flying Ants," "Snow Drifts into Tipis," and "Moon of the Strong Cold." Now known as Kmitxaɫtitnam, or "Shooting Month," because of the tradition introduced by the fur traders of shooting guns at the moon to welcome in the New Year.

Midwinter would find the Kootenai people, since time immemorial, gathered at what is now Apgar campground on the west side of Glacier. The people gathered to sing and dance as the spirits had taught them at the beginning of time, in order to have good health, good journeys, and food to sustain them. There, by the shores of Lake McDonald, the people returned every year at midwinter to their winter headquarters for this important gathering and renewal ceremony. Thousands of people, well-stocked with foods that they had dried during the summer and fall, also brought in fresh deer meat and fish. Our elders remember that so many people gathered to dance and sing these songs of their ancestors that dust would be raised, even though the first snow had fallen!

Winter camps required shelter from the wind, a good supply of fuel, cottonwood bark to feed the horses when grasses were buried by deep snow, and a source of fish. The men hunted nearby because animals sought out the same protected valleys. Individual hunters sometimes stalked deer

The Place Where They Dance

IN the middle of that first winter, the people were camped at a place we call *Ya· kiɫ Haqwiɫnamki.* (Today, that location is called Apgar, a campground in Glacier Park.) The wintertime came, and in the middle of the winter, this spirit came. He told one of the people who made contact with this spirit what they were to do to help themselves on their trail throughout the year. "You sing these three songs, and you sing them in this order. This first song is for your good health, the second song is for food so you'll have plenty of food to eat, and the third song is for material possessions.

"When you sing each of these songs you are to dance in a circle, and that circle is going to represent your road for the coming year. . . . When you're half-way around [the circle], it will be in the middle of summertime, and when you get back around to where you started from, it will be in the middle of next winter. What you'll be doing when you sing those songs and dance in a circle, you'll be putting good health, plenty of food, and material possessions on your road until the middle of next winter.

"The circle represents the road that you're going to walk, from right now in the middle of the wintertime and until the middle of the next winter. Everything will cycle through from the spring to summer to fall and back to winter again. And that circle will represent your road, and what you'll be asking for is that your road be good and you get back here to this spot again in the middle of next winter."

And so that's what the people did. They sang the songs and danced in a circle. And then throughout the year, sure enough, good things were put on their trail. So, in the middle of the next winter, there they were again, camped there in the same place. Again, they sang the songs and they danced there. So in the middle of the wintertime, the next year, there they were again. So they came to call that place Ya· kiɫ Haqwiɫnamki—"The Place Where They Dance."

I was told that the 'Aqɫsmaknik, the Kootenai, camped at that same spot, that was their winter camp, and they danced for the next ten thousand generations. And that spirit helped them on their road throughout those years. Then in 1910 a gentleman by the name of Apgar came along and decided he wanted his homestead at that particular site. And he didn't want all of these 'Aqɫsmaknik coming and dancing there in the middle of the wintertime. So after ten thousand generations, the 'Aqɫsmaknik were told that they couldn't go back to that spot to dance. That's when they moved the dance down to the reservation, where it takes place inside a nice climate-controlled building.

So, the real name of what has been known for one hundred years as Apgar was known for ten thousand generations as Ya· kiɫ Haqwiɫnamki, The Place Where They Dance. There have been millions of 'Aqɫsmaknik who have died in this area. They have turned into the earth that's here, and some of the blood that is going through my veins was there at that first winter camp, and that connection is felt by all of the Kootenai people.

—As told by Vernon Finley, Kootenai educator

Lake McDonald in winter T. J. Hileman, photographer, Schultz Collection, Merrill G. Burlingame Special Collections, Montana State University Libraries, Bozeman, 222

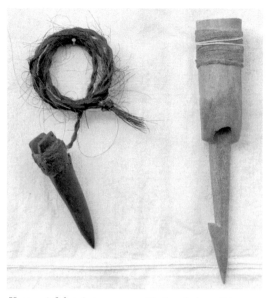

Kootenai fish points, ca. 1935 Glenbow Archives, Calgary, Alberta, Canada, NA-5213-131

wearing a deerskin robe and a deer's head upon their own, with the ears arranged to stand erect. These methods helped them to sneak right up to the deer unnoticed. Men, aided by dogs, pursued elk on snowshoes. They worked in teams to trap the elk in deep snow, so they could be brought down with an arrow in the early days, and later with a bullet.

Winter fishing for trout and whitefish was done through the ice with hook and line, using grubs for bait, which were found inside rotten stumps. Upon breaking the stump open, people would find these white grub worms, remembered by elders as being "as big as your finger." The Kootenai name for this creature means "feces trail," for the track left behind in the pine stump. On the end of a hook, the grubs served as good bait.

Fish as a food source were more important before people acquired horses and firearms, both of which made buffalo easier to hunt. However, fish always provided variety and nutrients not found elsewhere.

Ling (burbot), an eel-like fish that grows to two feet and larger, was a dependable food source, and it was especially important for the Lower Kootenais. In late January and early February, "ling move in schools from the Kootenai river up the different tributaries," where they were caught in traps as they ascended the small streams. Elders told Claude Schaeffer the details of trapping this fish, which was taken at night: "Since the streams

Fish trap (reproduction) Courtesy Tim Ryan

were frozen over at this season, it was necessary to break through the ice with a stone maul in order to set the weir and trap. . . . The trap was lowered into position at night and examined the following morning. Often from twenty to thirty ling were caught during one night."[1]

Each day the fresh ice was cleared away from the trap area. If warmer weather and rainfall brought about a rise in the stream and threatened the breakup of the ice, the traps were removed to prevent their destruction. Ling fishing was done by individual families, and not as a community activity.

Ideally, for winter sustenance, the people managed to bring in fresh meat to eat alongside their dried foods of venison, fish, berries, and roots. This variety helped maintain important nutritional balance. Huckleberries and other dried fruits would be rejuvenated by boiling, either alone or with dried roots. Dried camas cakes were another important winter food source.

Winter was the time to collect willow and dogwood for making fish traps and other items. These materials need to be collected when their moisture content is low, in order for the bindings to hold when they're lashed together. Think of trying to saddle a horse when its lungs are full of air. Similarly, if the branches are tied together when the moisture content is high, the lashings become loose as the branches dry out.

Red osier dogwood
Jacqueline Moore, artist

These winter camps were cozy. The preferred covering for winter lodges was the hide of elk. The hearths in each family lodge were kept burning, fed by dried wood that had been gathered by women and children. To make a fire, two people would whirl a stick about two feet long, set in a hole in a slab of softer wood, such as cottonwood. The friction would cause the wood to ignite, and the sparks were then helped along by kindling. The people carried a punk, or "slow match," with them. They would keep dry bark smoldering inside clamshells covered with buckskin. They also kept fire alive by covering coals with earth and later digging into the middle of the ashes and blowing on them to reignite the flame. Cottonwood was a good fuel for tipi fires, as it produces little smoke. Inside a heated lodge in a sheltered valley, life was good, regardless of the weather.

Nupqu Natanik (February), or "The Time That Bear Cubs Are Born"

Also known as "Moon of the Snowblind

By the last of January or first of February, it was time to set out on the winter hunt. Predictably, most of the winter snow had fallen, early winter winds had receded, and the people could expect a period of clear weather. Usually by that time, deep snow became traversable. A warm spell would melt the surface of the snow, and when it turned cold again, a crust formed on the surface. These conditions allowed the Kootenais to go longer distances on snowshoes. Once the crust had formed on the snow, the people were ready to go "over the humps" for buffalo.

Our ancestors had been conducting this winter hunt since the days before they acquired horses. Long ago, at least one Kootenai band ran buffalo over shallow cliffs and into corrals where they were shot with arrows. The name for these buffalo pens was *akulala*. In later years, buffalo were driven into snowdrifts, where hunters with bow and arrows, and later with guns, were waiting for them.

Hunting on snowshoes *Personal Recollections and Observations of General Nelson A. Miles . . .* (Chicago: Werner, 1897), 128

This winter hunt was necessary to get enough food for the thousands of Kootenais gathered together at The Dancing Place. It was a good time to travel because the Blackfeet were settled in their winter camps and not watching the eastern fringe of the high country for enemies. So confident were these Kootenai hunters that they didn't even post guards.

If the loons showed no signals of approaching storms, the hunting parties would prepare to leave. For some hunts, only the young and able-bodied traveled eastward over the Rockies, leaving older people and young children back at the main camp, where they continued to fish for food. At other times, whole families, including babies, would go for food.

Traveling guidance and leadership in camp were the responsibility of men who had earned respect in these realms. The travel leader was chosen on the basis of his knowledge of trails and good camp locations. This role changed for winter and summer travel. Winter leaders needed to understand snow and avalanche conditions, winter camp locations, and best travel routes on snowshoes.

The Winter Hunt

▶ ▶ ▶ ▶ ▶ ▶ ▶ ◈ ◀ ◀ ◀ ◀ ◀ ◀ ◀

THE size of the winter bison hunting party varied from two or three families to as many as ten or twelve families (10 to 150 individuals). Some preferred to take one route or go to one area, while other people differed. Dry meat and a small quantity of bitterroot were taken for food by a hunting party. Camas was too heavy to be packed. If dry meat was lacking, the party attempted to live on birds on route.

When the Kutenai travelled eastward on foot, they camped in the thick timber. Then the camp circle was not used. The snow was deep and there was slight danger.

The party travelling eastward sent out scouts ahead to look for bison. If bison were seen at a great distance and none near at hand, a magical device (fat from small stomach) was thrown into fire to bring snow and cold weather, and thus bring bison into the shelter of the foothills.

—From the Schaeffer Papers

The men wore leggings (hair inside) and moccasins (hair inside), a buckskin shirt, and a short, cape-like robe of the "belly-skin" of the buffalo or the elk hide. Women wore a dress, leggings, and moccasins. Both sexes wore fur caps of beaver or muskrat. All wore bear-paw snowshoes. They rubbed charcoal around their eyes to protect them from the glare caused by the reflection of sunlight off the snow. Each person carried one blanket made from a partial buffalo robe. Their winter moccasins, made especially for snowshoes, were made of elk or caribou hide with hair inside.

The winter travelers were able to pack lightly because they would have cached food from their fall hunt high in trees along the trail. Instead of

Tobacco Plains Band leader Red Horn (Chief Paul David) Schultz Collection, Merrill G. Burlingame Special Collections, Montana State University Libraries, Bozeman, 287

having dogs pull tipi poles, they made simple lodge frames for temporary housing and covered them with flat cedar or hemlock boughs. They traveled during the late morning and early afternoon when the snow was crusted. Trailbreakers were sent ahead to prepare the trail.

One story told to Claude Schaeffer by Chief Paul David of the Tobacco Plains Band helps us to understand the knowledge and great responsibilities required of the travel leaders. These events started at Lake McDonald on a morning in early winter in the 1860s or 1870s. That morning all the hunters had followed the leader as they went up along the creeks. At one point, they sat down and the leader told them some would hunt along one creek and some along the other.

Paul was one of a party who moved up creek to Avalanche Lake. This trail was very high and steep; there was no timber at all and everything was covered with snow. Paul sat down to rest and the hunters moved on ahead. In a short time, Paul's friend came along and asked him

> why he did not move ahead. Paul said he didn't think it worthwhile, as it looked dangerous. They talked awhile and presently heard an avalanche across on cliffs opposite. Soon . . . [an] older Indian came along. [He] moved along the edge of the snowfield to where a few trees were standing and Paul and his friend heard a noise. [Looking up, . . . they saw the snow start . . . downwards toward them. The older Indian ran to a tree and encircled [it] with his arms and legs. Paul and his friend started to run; the friend for the timber and Paul ran downwards on the snowfield. No sooner had Paul reached the edge of the snowfield and gained the timber, than the avalanche swept past him.[2]

While traveling in the high country on their way to buffalo, hunters took advantage of opportunities to kill bighorn sheep and goats. They would climb above the bighorns and drive them into drifts below, where others were ready to dispatch them with knives or spears. For goats, they would follow them onto rocky ledges where they would be shot. Goats are easier to drag along because their silky hair does not catch in the snow.

They also hunted elk. The same conditions that enabled the hunters to move about with more ease restricted the mobility of elk and deer, whose thin legs would cut through the icy crust. On one of these hunts, according to a story recorded by Claude Schaeffer, a Kootenai had fallen behind the travel group when, upon entering a canyon in a bushy place, he saw some elk on a side hill. He killed an elk and started to butcher it, when

> looking through his legs, he saw three Piegan down below, sneaking up on him. He continued to tie up his pack, put it on his back, and went uphill away from the enemy. He feigned not to see them. He planned that if they continued to approach, he would drag his pack, double back and advance on the Piegans, who were already in snow up to their knees. They refused to advance farther as they realized they were out of the depth. The Kutenai then caught up with his party.[3]

Generally, during the winter hunt, travelers stayed in the shelter provided along the fringe of the foothill forests, except when the men left to hunt. In the best of circumstances, buffalo would be found near the passes and close to trails. A group of young men would be sent ahead to scout around for buffalo. If unsuccessful, the hunting party had to travel until buffalo were seen, always mindful of the distance they would have to pack meat back home.

The winter buffalo hunt used strategies similar to those used for elk hunting this time of year. The hunters would drive the buffalo into snow-drifts, then kill them. Some hunters were able to drive small herds within range by merely directing their movements by means of a robe. A fast runner was able to run alongside a running herd and turn them in the desired direction. A less common method was to use dogs to drive the buffalo onto a river or lake ice.

While on the eastern side of the mountains, people took advantage of ice fishing on the big lakes such as Two Medicine and St. Mary, especially if finding buffalo was taking longer than hoped for. To keep warm,

Bull elk Glacier National Park, HPF 8348

a fisherman knelt or sat upon fir boughs with a blanket placed over his head. The blanket also helped him to see into the water.

Pete Kiyiel [Caye], who was eighty years old in 1952 when interviewed by anthropologist Carling Malouf, remembered going on one of these winter treks over the mountains. He went with his parents when he was about eight years old and recalled that once they were on the other side, a few men continued on to the prairies and then drove the game animals back to the other men who were hidden in the foothills. These animals were chased and driven into snowdrifts where they were killed. Bows and arrows with small points were used to kill them.[4]

Once the hunters were successful, the women cut up the meat and separated out the bones, which were boiled separately to collect the grease. The people would feast on fresh meat and organs and then the women would go to work making dry meat for winter stores. The meat was smoked on a rack over a hot fire inside a small lodge. When almost dry, after about a day, the meat was condensed by pounding it with a stone hammer. Dried meat of one buffalo or two good-sized deer would fill a parfleche.

While the meat dried, people played games, visited, and practiced marksmanship. They made small grass figures of an elk, about five inches long. About a dozen of these figures were placed in a row about fifteen or twenty feet away, and young boys would practice shooting at them. A few of the figures were marked on the back with a purple or blue grass stem to represent fat cows. These would be mixed up among the others so that those shooting would not know their location. The boy hitting a "fat cow" was considered a good marksman. The older people played this game also; however, it was a game only played east of the mountains.[5]

Grass animal figure (reproduction) Courtesy Tim Ryan

There was never a game that didn't teach some kind of survival skill. The boys learned skills of hunting and warfare, with an emphasis on strength, good aim, and dexterity. Girls learned the skills and dexterity required for their lifework, such as sewing and hide tanning.

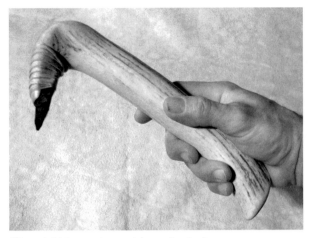

Women's hide-scraping tool (reproduction) Courtesy Tim Ryan

According to Paul David, if the chinook wind came while the Kootenais were in their winter hunting camp,

> then men and boys would divide into equal sides and each make a lot of snowballs. One side asked the other, 'Have you enough snowballs?' If the other had, the fight would start. The two sides lined up in two rows opposite each other, and one boy after another, until three had run, from one side, would run, dodging and twisting between the rows while one side tried to hit him with snowballs. If none were hit, three boys of the other side tried. When three boys of one side were 'killed,' that side lost.[6]

Once the meat was dried and packed, the hardest work for these winter hunters came when hauling their full packs back across the mountains. Chief Paul David described the process to Claude Schaeffer:

> Men packed from 30–40 lbs and only one could pack 50 lbs. A married woman could pack 18 lbs and a younger girl (15–18 years), 8 lbs. In breaking camp the five or six leaders who broke the trail would not carry packs because they broke the trail through the snow. This was on the bison range. One would break trail for a quarter mile or more and would then step aside; another would

then act as trail breaker, and the rest would alternate in turn. Each would step into the rear place during his rest walking. The leaders wore snowshoes and were the largest, strongest men.[7]

Pete Caye shared other details of this method of transport with Carling Malouf: "We packed the meat back in relays. One man would go a mile and a half with a big pack on his back, then another would take it on, to be relieved still later by another man still farther on. We could pack a lot more that way."[8]

Ambrose Gravelle described for Claude Schaeffer the design and method for carrying the packs home from these winter hunts: "The heavy packs were usually supported by two back straps, one horizontally across the breast and shoulders and the second passing horizontally across the forehead. These were made of goat, elk or bison hide. They were about 3" wide at the center tapering down to 1" towards the ends. They were from 6–7 feet long."[9]

According to Gravelle, the maximum distance between two campsites was about ten miles: that was the most people could manage, with men carrying two parfleches of eighteen to nineteen pounds each, and women carrying one.

> Bison or elk hides were turned hair side out and spread on the ground. Three bundles of dried meat were placed on the hide, folded over and securely tied. The pack was then about 8 feet long and 3 or more feet wide. The packs could then be eased down a long snow slide over two miles long. The people would descend to the bottom of [the] declivity by a less-steep, roundabout way to the bundles of dried meat. . . .
>
> The children and old women would wear snowshoes and the latter would carry a small pack, not very wide, and older girls would pack small babies in hide bags. The small bags carried the cooking equipment, such as pots, etc.[10]

At least one time, a returning hunting party crafted elk-skin canoes as a way to ferry the meat homeward. During the winter buffalo hunt described by Paul David, after surviving the avalanche, this Tobacco Plains Band traveled back from the South Fork of the Two Medicine River over Marias Pass, then to the South Fork of the Flathead River, now within the Bob Marshall Wilderness south of Glacier. There they met some Lower Kootenai hunters who were preparing two canoes to transport their elk hides back home. This strategy looked like a good one to the tired hikers. The Tobacco Plains hunting party traded buffalo meat and hides to the Lower Kootenais in exchange for some elk hides to make another canoe, which they did with help from the Lower Kootenais. Together, they packed their equipment and belongings in the canoes and proceeded homeward. The men went by canoe, while the women and children traveled by snowshoes along the river.

Upon return to the Tobacco Plains from the buffalo range, the hunters would cache their packs of dried meat in conifer trees, where it would be waiting for them when next they crossed the mountains. Their next stop was then to move to the Yahk country west of the Kootenay River in southern British Columbia, where they would hunt caribou.[11]

Łikuq (March), or "Melting Snow Starts Flowing"

Also known as the "Leaf Bud Moon"

The time before the spring greens emerged was known as the period of scarcity. When dried stores were nearly gone and fresh food was unavailable, especially if the winter hunts had been unsuccessful, people might go hungry. This was when dried meat was crucial. In periods of scarcity, moss was boiled with the stomach contents, or even the droppings, of the "fool hen" (spruce grouse) for added flavor and nutrients.

To supplement their meager stores, the Kootenais fished for suckers. These bony bottom-dwellers were only eaten in times of need. They were taken with spears, hook and line, and also in traps.

At the end of the winter season, if they were in dire need of surviving, then they'd go ahead and get what they needed, even though this was breaking a food taboo. It was, and continues to be, against our way to take animals when they are carrying young, but you did what you needed when this was the only way to survive. Under such circumstances, if a female deer was seen, before the animal was killed, the hunter would say a prayer of cleansing to prepare for breaking this natural law. Once the animal was killed, absolutely everything that could be eaten was consumed, even the guts and ears. Nothing could go to waste.

During this quiet time before plants burst from the ground and animals emerged from slumber, many tasks kept people busy in camp. Women made sure that clothes for their families were in good shape and that new lodge covers were ready. They also completed new parfleches made from the thick winter hides of buffalo. Men and women repaired or replaced any tools they would need for the upcoming season. Men showed boys how to straighten arrows made from serviceberry shoots and how to carve bows from yew and other hardwoods.

Yawuki· kam, "Comes-From-Down-Below," was responsible for bringing the gift of the all-important serviceberry to the people. As told long ago, this mythic hero went to the place in the world where serviceberries grew, gathered shoots to make his arrows, and then planted serviceberries in many places so there would be enough for arrows when people came into the world. From ducks, he obtained feathers for his arrows; from the horn of mountain sheep, he made an arrow straightener. And from a bull moose, he obtained sinew with which to attach the feathers on his arrows.

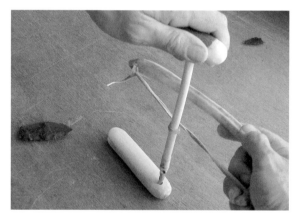

Kootenai-style hand drill (reproduction) Courtesy Tim Ryan

Worn-out drills were used by children to practice drilling holes in wood, soft stone, and seeds. Fish spears, hooks, and traps were made ready for the spring fishing that would start as soon as the snowmelt began. Women worked with girls to prepare a good supply of sinew and rope and straps from fibers of dogbane and other plants. They had sharp new needles and awls tucked away in their sewing kits. People decorated their clothing with beads, quills, and other objects, and painted the parfleche bags.

A new supply of tule provided the material for lodge covers, work surfaces, and anything else you would use a mat for. Tule is a wonderful material for a lodge in certain seasons. When it's cold and wet, the tule

(opposite) Model Kootenai lodge made of tule mats (reproduction) Courtesy Tim Ryan

expands, keeping out the wind. When the weather is hot and dry, the reeds condense and allow a breeze to flow through the lodge. Skin lodges are better than tule mats for cold and dry weather.

In this season, prayers were offered for the health and prosperity of the tribe and the success of the upcoming deer hunt.

Kaḱkmi (April), or "Cracks Begin to Form in the Ground"

Also known as the "Moon of the Big Leaves," "Moon of the Red Grass Appearing," and "Moon of Making Fat"

Spring was the season when bears came out of their caves, hungry for many of the same roots that fed the people. Children were taught to be careful about how they talked about bears and what they called them. Many teachings come from bears.

Migratory birds, especially ducks, swans, cranes, and geese, provided good variety to the spring diet. A group activity was to scare ducks off the water and then to catch them in a net. Picture a lightweight, portable soccer goal. Leo Williams remembers that two people would hold the light poles with a net stretched in between while another person would drive the ducks in that direction. When the ducks started flying low above the ground, after running along the water, the people would catch them in the net.[12]

Eggs were treasured. Female geese start laying eggs during the first weeks of March and continue as late as June, and ducks lay their eggs around the same time. Canada geese typically nest on the ground on islands and shorelines, laying about six eggs, one per day. Males are very aggressive in protecting the nest, making egg collecting a potentially dangerous activity. Duck nests, although more difficult to find, are easier to rob.

Wood ducks nest in trees, generally near water. They are very secretive about their nests, making them hard to find, but these nests can some-times yield a bounty of up to forty eggs because of the practice of "egg dumping." Mixed broods are common in waterfowl, occurring when a female loses her nest during her egg-laying period and must "dump" her eggs in another nest, where a foster parent will incubate them.

Mallards usually build their nests on the ground, often in marshes or among bulrushes of swampy creeks, or even in the hollow of a tree. A hen

Kootenai duck hunter, 1910 E. S. Curtis, photographer, Library of Congress, LC-USZ62-46999

mallard will lay one egg a day until the clutch is complete with about eight to ten eggs. Then she will begin to incubate the eggs for about one moon cycle. Kootenais would carefully observe the nest and approach when the adults were away. They would take one egg and mark the others with charcoal so they could keep track of which new eggs to collect in the following days. Collecting a few eggs doesn't diminish the duck population because the female continues to lay eggs until the clutch is full.

Early spring was a time when people could catch whitefish with their bare hands. Vernon Finley explains that when you stood in the shallow water of a lake where a river was feeding in near the reeds, the water was dirty from the snowmelt coming in, but people could feel the whitefish bumping up against their legs and could grab them and throw them out of the water. The northwest side of Flathead Lake (Somers) was a favorite place to take fish this way. Depending on the take and the need, some of the fish, along with their roe, were dried separately and stored for future use. The inlet of Lake McDonald provided a similar opportunity for late winter fishing.

Arrowleaf balsamroot stems provided a fresh treat, somewhat like celery. Fresh greens were especially appreciated after the long winter. The

Arrowleaf balsamroot
Jacqueline Moore, artist

tender new shoots of balsamroot also provide important food for deer and elk in the spring.

With the receding snow, antlers shed the previous fall were gathered for many useful purposes. Some of the important tools included the antler-handled digging sticks women used for roots, and the antler knapping tools that men used for making knives and projectile points for hunting.

U·ɫumi (May), or "Water Starts to Rise"

Also known as the "Moon When Ponies Shed"

Our Kootenai elders were proactive in their efforts to get fresh meat after the lean period of late winter. They took the initiative to burn the prairies to stimulate growth of grasses as a way to attract elk. In early May 1808, while camped with Kootenais, David Thompson's crew followed this example by setting ground fires to clear the brush and stimulate new growth.

Fish were important year-round. Men caught the fish, brought them to camp, and prepared the fire. During the first couple of days, people ate as much fresh fish as they desired. Fish were boiled in baskets with water heated by red-hot rocks. The rocks were transferred from fire to water, using two sticks, held like a vise. According to Simon Francis, "When the fish were served, the group sat in a big circle by families. The chief was considered the head of the table. Fish were first served to him and then down the line on each side. The places on his right and left were the honor positions. If there was an assistant chief, he sat by the chief.[13]

Anything not consumed had to be processed quickly. The women cut the fish in such a way that they could be hung up to dry within a couple of hours. Industrious women rendered fat from oily fish and stored it in a receptacle made of a deer's bladder. With such a lean diet, fish oil was an important addition.

Kootenais also fished for sucker and ling at tributary mouths. During the spring runoff, ling were taken by a three-pronged spear from a canoe by torchlight at night. The spear's center prong was made out of a lower deer leg, and the side prongs were made of serviceberry wood. They would fasten a foreshaft to a ten-inch shaft with sinew. One way to make a torch was with a roll of peeled birch bark, held on a stick.

The sweet inner bark and sap of the black cottonwood is even sweeter than that of the ponderosa. Trees are peeled in May when the sap is running. In addition to scraping the bark to remove sheets of cambium, our ancestors would hollow a portion of the trunk to collect the sap for eating.

Fishing from a Kootenai canoe R. H. McKay, photographer, Archives and Special Collections, Mansfield Library, University of Montana, Missoula, 94.1902

Spring Fishing

IN the 1950s, Simon Francis, from the Lower Kootenai Bonner's Ferry Band, told anthropologist Paul Baker about the way they used to conduct their spring fishing expeditions:

> In the spring after the river had overflowed the meadows, the fish were out in sloughs and ponds. At the places where the water made its way back to the river, traps would be set to catch the fish as they sought deeper water. It was at this time that men, women, and children went out to get their spring catch. Tepees were set up for each family, generally in a circle for social purposes and for protection. The campfire was built in the middle of the circle.
>
> After the camp was set up and before the traps were set, there was an all night ritual of singing, chanting, and dancing. It was a religious ceremony that helped to guarantee a successful catch.
>
> According to Simon, it was "to look unto your power to see that everything was all right. If other people, enemies, had set up bad medicine, then this ritual would destroy it." The singing and chanting ceremony continued until midnight the second and third nights. The chief of the tribe generally presided at these ceremonies.
>
> The morning after the first night of singing the men went out to set the traps. One man or a group of men skilled in the arts of fishing directed the effort. The fish were brought to camp in bark boxes or baskets. By the end of the first day there was a large catch. The fish were put in piles of equal size, one for each family. This task of dividing the fish was generally carried through by the small boys of the tribe. Visitors, newcomers, strangers received an equal share with all the rest. . . . The catch was free and, therefore, all should share equally in it.

—Excerpted from Baker, *Forgotten Kutenai,* 31

*Kootenai fish spear
(reproduction)*
Courtesy Tim Ryan

This time of year might find some Kootenais extracting bark from the enormous western red cedar trees that were common up Avalanche Creek. Cedar was a highly valued and important construction material because of its qualities of lightness and durability. Cedar also provided the light and buoyant material for canoe frames, which were then covered with elk skin, birch bark, or bark of white pine, depending on where the Kootenais were and what resources were available. In the mountains, elk hides were more commonly used.

Huge bowls for feasts were created by burning out a downed cedar tree. Both ends would be burned and a fire set on top to hollow out the shape. The fire also hardened the wood, providing a seal.[14]

Paper birch grows in the same habitat as cedar and provided many important gifts for the people to use. The flaky outer bark was used as tinder for starting fires. The peeled inner bark, in addition to serving as the material for a night-light, provided a wonderful resource for making baskets. These containers could be made waterproof by coating them with pitch from a conifer, which would make them serviceable for carrying water or for use as cooking pots. Water could be made to boil by adding fire-heated rocks to the basket.

During this same season, when bark is easy to separate from the tree, people harvested cedar bark and roots for other types of baskets. They split the fine roots in two and peeled them. The split roots formed two sizes of fiber, larger ones for coils and smaller ones to sew the coils together. The women sewed and bound two strands alternately around the coil to make the baskets firm and tightly woven so they were watertight for cooking. Sometimes they dyed the fibers black and green—black from wild carrot root and green from a type of mountain grass.

Tools for making baskets included needles made from the lower front leg bones of deer and awls from the deer's thicker upper leg bones. The fibrous bark of wolf willow provided another good material for baskets and rope. Late spring was the ideal time to collect this fiber, when it was easy to separate the bark from the stem.

Shoots, greens, and bulbs emerged with vigor after the snow melted. The official root-gathering season opened with the ripening of bitterroot in May. At this time, the large, fleshy taproots were most tender and nutritious, containing their highest starch content before the flowers bloomed. Bitterroot is not widespread in Kootenai Country, but it was (and is) a highly valued food, nonetheless. These roots are extremely nutritious, and the dried food is lightweight for portability.

Basketmaking tool (reproduction) Courtesy Tim Ryan

Root gathering has always been done by the women, and it is done in a sacred manner. The people understand that they depend on the nourishment of this annual staple, and they are very careful to express gratitude and to take care of this important food gift. The season is initiated each year by a simple, first-fruits ceremony led by a respected woman. The people wait for this official opening of the bitterroot season, when the lead woman determines it is the right time to harvest the roots. This lead woman is chosen by the elders on the basis of her knowledge and character, and she holds the position for life. In this role, she takes on a big responsibility for the good of the community.

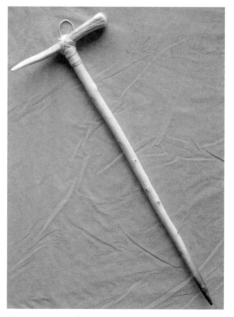

Digging stick (reproduction) Courtesy Tim Ryan

Bitterroot Jacqueline Moore, artist

In the old days, before the digging began, the chief prayed for the safety of the gatherers, then these women took their digging sticks, baskets, and parfleche bags to the root grounds. A few men served as guards against the attack of enemies or grizzlies. After the first bitterroot had been ceremoniously gathered by the lead woman and prayers had been said, the first bitterroot was peeled and turned over to the leader, who carried it back with her to be placed in the chief's lodge. When this annual ritual had been completed, the women were free to dig roots for their family's use. They worked together; some would dig while others peeled off the outer brownish-red covering of the root and removed the source of the bitter taste, the red "heart."

The following day, after prayers of thanksgiving were shared, the people feasted on bitterroot boiled in broth from the flesh of blue grouse and deer. After the feast, the different families scattered to various bitterroot sites in order to acquire a large supply. While women were digging and processing the roots for future use, the men hunted deer. Gathering and processing the roots took several days. Each family tried to gather as much as possible for use during the coming winter. Digging was hard work, and most areas had only scattered plants, requiring several days of labor to gather a winter's supply. After digging and peeling, the roots were

Biscuitroot
Jacqueline Moore, artist

spread out on a hide to dry in the sun for one or two days, depending on conditions. Once dry, they were packed in parfleche bags and cached upon tree platforms. Two ordinary parfleches of the dried roots, eaten sporadically, would last two people through the winter.

Girls enjoyed a jumping game during this season of the bitterroot. As remembered by Mrs. Tom and recorded by Claude Schaeffer, "Girls would bend over so that their knees nearly touched their chin, and would then jump up and down on the balls of both feet. They formed a circle and the one who could last the longest won." In another game in honor of the bitterroots, girls would seat themselves in two rows, about thirty feet away from each other, "with their legs outstretched before them on the ground. A girl would walk forward toward the other row, eyes closed, slowly clapping her hands saying *ka-la* (meaning 'Who?')." Those seated in the row responded to her question with the word *kamin*, meaning "Me." Following the sound of a voice, the "seeker," the girl with closed eyes, finally came in contact with someone of this group, who would then climb upon the seeker's back, with her head downward and her legs bent over the shoulders of the seeker, who remained standing. The seeker held the other girl's legs behind her neck and then whirled her around and around. One exclaimed, "Snake, snake," referring to the digging stick and the other replied, "Frog, frog," which referred to the bark berry basket.[15]

Bitterroot and camas both grow in the southern part of Kootenai territory and were the main root crops that provided dried provisions for the winter, but many other roots, shoots, and greens were relished this time of year.

Indian potatoes, or spring beauty, are crisp corms about the size of your thumb that can be eaten fresh or boiled like potatoes. They grow from the lower foothills up mountain slopes all the way to high alpine meadows, frequently in snowbanks, providing a long gathering season as people moved into the mountains following elk, deer, and berries.

Young leaves of arrowleaf balsamroot could be eaten raw or steamed, and the large root was also eaten. According to ethnobotanist Nancy Turner, these roots were dug "just as the leaves began to show above the ground. They could also be dug later, but became stringy as the plants matured. They were beaten to loosen the tough outer skin, then peeled, and the white inner part steam-cooked overnight . . . [and] eaten immediately or threaded on a string or stick and dried."[16]

Biscuitroot is a tasty and popular root that was harvested in the spring. Kootenais sometimes ate the roots raw but usually baked them in a pit for several hours. Yellowbell bulbs also provided a tasty treat around this time as well. They were washed, boiled, and eaten. They are relatively difficult to dig and don't grow in enough quantity to merit drying and storing them.

The stalk of wild rhubarb, or cow parsnip, was collected, stripped of leaves, and thrown into a fire to roast. Once cooked, the outer layer was

Yellowbells
Jacqueline Moore, artist

removed and eaten. The people used a mixture of tallow and wild rhubarb root to make rawhide rope soft. They also used the hollow stem for an elk call. The Kootenais refer to water hemlock as "poison wild rhubarb."

Quartz Creek, a tributary of the North Fork of the Flathead River in Glacier Park, had two "wild rhubarb" place names. "Where Rhubarb Is Long" is the name for Lower Quartz Lake, and "Head of Rhubarb" is Quartz Lake. Sperry Glacier was known as "Wild Rhubarb Blossom Ice." When asked if Quartz Creek had an abundance of wild rhubarb, Vernon Finley explained that Wild Rhubarb was also a son of Coyote, noting that Sperry Glacier is also called Coyote's Son Ice. Sperry Glacier is not within the same drainage, so perhaps the Quartz Creek references are actually to a place where wild rhubarb was gathered.

The Kootenais had multiple tobacco garden areas, including one south of Polebridge in what today is Glacier Park and another near Spotted Bear in what is now the Bob Marshall Wilderness, to the south of Glacier Park. Whereas women were responsible for harvesting plant foods, men planted and tended tobacco. They would plant the seeds before the summer buffalo hunt. Runners would return off and on all summer to hoe and weed the tobacco plots, then return to hunting camps.

While men were planting tobacco and hunting, the women would acquire new tipi poles. Being dragged back and forth over the mountains would wear the poles down, so new ones would be required. May was the best time to gather them because that's when they're easy to peel. Women cut the poles with antler axes, then peeled the poles, leaving them to dry in the sun. Lodgepole pines provided the perfect frame for a tipi, as the poles are remarkably strong, yet light, and they are abundantly available.

Kootenai Lodge Covers

▸ ▸ ▸ ▸ ▸ ▸ ▸   ◈   ◂ ◂ ◂ ◂ ◂ ◂ ◂

KOOTENAI tipis today are not painted as they were years ago. The Kootenai Indians painted animals and birds on their tipis. The kind of animal painted on a tipi meant the owner's spirit was like that particular animal. It may have been a bear, deer, buffalo, or some other animal or bird.

Some tipis were painted with a ripple design, a symbol of green grass. Other designs were mainly for decorative purposes, more or less to beautify the tipi.

—Adapted from the Kootenai Culture Committee's *How Marten Got His Spots*, n. p.

Traveling along their well-worn trails, the people would arrive at their familiar spring camps, knowing they would find many bulky objects they had left behind the previous year. This lifestyle required light travel, so they didn't want to carry heavy tools, such as berry mashers, or pestles, when not needed. They might also have left some good tipi poles, heavy mauls and axes, and other tools too heavy to carry from camp to camp. Pestles and other grinding stones are often found stashed at the edge of a camp area abandoned long ago. A number of these tools have been found along the prairie edges in the North Fork and along lakeshores on the east side of the divide.

Kuǫukupku (June), or "Moon of Strawberries Ripening"

Also known as "Moon When Green Grass Is Up"

Camas follows bitterroot, and the Kootenais would switch from one to the other toward the end of May. There are two varieties of camas, one smaller than the other. Both types were important sources of food that were dug in quantities, then dried, roasted, and stored for the winter. The fact that they store so well is one reason they were so highly valued. They have a potato-like flavor. Kootenai women know that white-flowered "death camas" can be distinguished from blue camas when not in bloom by the green or yellow glands that occur at the base of each of the flower petals of the toxic variety. The roots of the death camas also differ from those of the edible camas. Women would actively remove the death camas from the camas fields.

Their camas-harvesting strategy was also a propagation strategy. By thinning the crop, the remaining bulbs could grow larger. When this relationship between the food and the people is maintained, the camas crop thrives. When they go without harvesting, the roots get small.

Each family took care of roasting and processing its own camas. They would line the bottom of a pit with stones and build a fire upon them to create coals. The camas was baked between layers of grass and other vegetation and then covered with a layer of earth. A little water could be directed upon the hot rocks by means of a hollow tube. For heat, a large fire was built on top of the pit and was kept burning for three days.

Camas roasting, like the digging, was women's work. Men weren't even allowed to be near the roasting pits, although they could renew the

Camas Jacqueline Moore, artist

supply of wood to keep the fire going. After three days of baking, the camas needed five or six days more to dry. Once the roots were ready, each woman took a portion to the chief, who offered a prayer before the cooked camas was served to the camp. The remainder was stored away for future use.

After the roots had been harvested in the lower valleys, it was time to follow the foods as they ripened at higher and higher elevations. The deer and elk followed the plant foods, and fish were abundant in mountain streams.

At this time, heads of households of several bands gathered at a pond near what is now Eureka, Montana, to decide plans for a buffalo hunt. A travel leader was selected—the person who, because of his knowledge, would be responsible for deciding where to go and when to leave. This summer travel leader had to know places for horses to feed, the best travel routes for horses, and places of potential ambush. He would send runners ahead to do reconnaissance, to report on rockslides, and to determine when the top of the selected pass would be free of snow. The number of lodges that would go on the hunt varied, depending on relationships with the Blackfeet and other circumstances, but these were large parties, consisting of 80 to 150 lodges, and included many hundred people and as many horses.

Imagine this scene of hundreds of people and horses heading toward the mountains, following the ripening foods. Each morning the "announcer" would give the chief's instructions for the day, and the camp would quickly mobilize. Men wore shirts, leggings, and breechcloths, and women wore dresses made of deerskin. In hot weather, both men and women went bare-legged and barefoot. Summer moccasins, generally used for "dress-up," were made of tanned deerskin decorated with quills and later with beadwork.

The North Fork of the Flathead offered many foods and other things needed at this time of year. If the snows were clear, the people might travel over the Grave Creek Trail from the Tobacco Plains to the Kintla Lake area of the North Fork, crossing the northwest corner of what is

Drawing of a buffalo hunt by Father Nicolas Point, 1842 Jesuit Archives: Central U.S., Saint Louis, Missouri, IX C 9,098

now within Glacier Park. If they were around Flathead Lake, they would travel to the Columbia Falls area and up the Flathead River to the Forks. All along the way, they enjoyed the fruits of the season.

Camas ripened later at higher elevations, extending the root-gathering season well into June and even July. En route, Kootenais would visit various camas fields in grassy areas along the South Fork of the Flathead River and along the North Fork within what is today Glacier Park as they moved into the mountains. Tree moss was roasted together with small camas—a layer of wet moss, a layer of camas, and so on.

To dig camas along the North Fork, where small camas was common, a group would pick their campsite where the number of mosquitoes was tolerable and where there was a good supply of deer, an abundance of wood to roast the camas, and a supply of tree moss to roast with camas. Claude Schaeffer was told that "as soon as a good source of fire-wood was reached, the women would cook the moss and camas while the men hunted deer." If mosquitoes were a nuisance, people would apply the juice from wet yarrow leaves to repel the pests.[17]

Yarrow Jacqueline Moore, artist

Kootenai fish trap Provincial Archives of British Columbia, *Kootenay* (British Columbia Provincial Museum: Victoria, B.C., 1952), 19

Late spring was a great time for fishing the tributaries of the North Fork. With the rising waters of the summer freshet, fish weirs of wicker-work screens were placed in the shallow, swift-flowing streams of the upriver country to capture bull trout and whitefish, among other species. These weirs were backed by a row of four-pole supports. These open-basket traps were tended throughout the night by relays of men.

Writing in *Forest and Stream* in the 1890s about some of the springtime wonders of Glacier, Charles Hallock listed the fish available at the outlet of Lake McDonald: "Belton is the starting point for Lake McDonald, a great body of water which fills a bottomless cleft right in the heart of the mountains, where big game of nearly all varieties may be found, and four varieties of trout running from 4 oz. to 30 lbs. in weight; black suckers, squaw fish and round whitefish, very palatable. At this season they gather at the inlet of the lake by myriads to spawn and the big trout feed on them."[18]

Fishing Goat Creek

▶ ▶ ▶ ▶ ▶ ▶ ▶ ◈ ◀ ◀ ◀ ◀ ◀ ◀ ◀

IN his 1890s article in *Field and Stream,* Charles Hallock reported that Goat Creek, the primary stream flowing into the north end of Lake McDonald, was

> swarming with small brook trout (*S. mykiss*) in the spring. . . . At this period of low water in the lake and streams the overflow is transparent. . . . In such gelid water mountain trout disport. The cream of trout fishing is from June 15 to the end of August. . . . During the spring freshets deep holes are formed in the channel, out of which barrels of beauties may be taken by any device that offers. In the fall they run into deep water and few are taken though I captured one with a trolling spoon at the edge of an offshore ledge in the lake which weighed a pound. At the same time bull trout marked with red and yellow spots seek the head of the lake where the inlet forms a gravelly shoal, . . . in pursuit of the round whitefish (*Coregonnus quadrilateralis*), which gather there in great numbers to spawn. Here also are found the squawfish, a species of small whitefish, the black sucker, and the red ribbon sucker, both of which grow to large size. The latter has a red stripe an inch wide extending along the lateral line from head to tail. Its back is dark brown and his belly white. To my taste the whitefish are the best flavored of all.
>
> —Excerpted from Hallock, "Marooning in High Altitudes," 488

When camas flowers reached full bloom in the meadows, cow elk had calved and mule deer were ready to give birth to fawns. Hallock noted that the Lake McDonald area was "a favorite camping ground for Flathead Indians [those from the Flathead Reservation], who make periodical visits to this location in quest of venison and buckskin, capturing hundreds of deer at each battue." ("Battue" refers to a method of driving game, where one group of people drives the game toward waiting hunters.)[19]

Vernon Finley explains that buckskin is at its best in the late spring and early summer "when the deer turn red." Finley's grandmother liked the hides for clothing best in July or when they had turned red. When tanned, the red hides turn very white, which is the preferred color. Earlier in the season, the hides are thinner and get holes in them easily, so they're not good to tan, and they are too hard to work. Hides are uneven, "like their scraggly looking selves at this time of year." Later in the season, when the red is gone and they're starting to turn gray, his grandmother didn't like to use them because the tanned hides would look gray. Kootenai women were known for their beautiful white buckskin hides. Deer hides "were like the denim of today."[20]

Many species of trees provided sweetness to the diet, either as cambium to chew or syrup to congeal and suck. Early summer was a time when the cambium layer was removed from the white and red pine with a deer rib or wooden scraper. Evidence of peeled trees extends all along the open prairies of the North Fork.

Syrup from larch trees is especially sweet. To obtain this syrup, Kootenais would hollow out a cavity in the trunk, allowing a large quantity of sap to accumulate, which they would gather once or twice a year. The larch also had medicinal properties. Kootenais applied the gum on cuts and bruises and made a tea from its bark for tuberculosis.

Eagle trapping was practiced by individuals. But this type of spiritual activity was very personal and wasn't shared with others. Accordingly, no details are available to report.

Kootenai woman dressing skins E. S. Curtis, *North American Indian . . . ,* vol. 7 (Cambridge, Mass.: privately published, 1911), 122, courtesy Mansfield Library, University of Montana, Missoula

Ponderosa pine with scar left when bark was peeled off to access the cambium inside Glacier National Park, HPF 2848

Chert was quarried up Bowman Creek, providing a new supply for the upcoming elk and buffalo hunts and for many other tools made from this "flakeable" stone. Bowman chert is found at archaeological sites throughout Kootenai territory, dating back some ten thousand years.

All of these North Fork activities were secondary to the late spring buffalo hunt that took people across the mountains. According to anthropologist Claude Schaeffer:

> The Kutenai did not travel eastward for bison during the summer before horses were introduced: they only went in winter when snow was deep. There was also danger in fording the mountain streams, during spring run-off period. Travel was easier on snowshoes in winter than travel in summer. This meant that they did not obtain summer hides for lodge covers and hence, their lodges

were made of brush and bark, and other products made from heavy winter hides.[21]

The Kootenais would be joined for this spring buffalo hunt by various peoples from other Columbia River basin tribes, including Coeur d'Alenes, Pend d'Oreilles, and Spokanes. The Akanahonek were few in numbers and did not own many horses, so that even during the summer hunt, they seldom ventured far out on the plains. However, after joining with other western tribes, they moved eastward in large numbers for the spring hunt, for now neither they nor, more particularly, the Akiyinik, needed to fear attack from the plains tribes. They moved out upon the plains as far as the Sweet Grass Hills (known to the Kootenais as Three Buttes). They left their camps at the time when the wild strawberries were ripening and went hunting for about a month.

En route to the bison chase, the party would stop, dismount, and an old man would offer a prayer. Then all remounted and continued. They would approach as near to the bison as possible—approximately six hundred yards—before the herd would come together and start running. The Kootenais, if alone, did not shout, which was a Salish and Pend d'Oreille practice, but the lead man would cry, "Ready." Then the hunters would ride close to the herd and begin shooting. Claude Schaeffer recorded Eneas Tallow's memory of the hunt:

> A mounted hunter could kill two or three animals before the herd disappeared. He would throw a quiver or any personal object on the animal to identify it as his and then ride after another animal. The hunter would then go back to butcher the animals and then return to camp for pack animals. Sometimes his wife or daughters would accompany him to help pack the meat to camp. It would take the average family a week to cut up and cure the meat of three buffalo. . . .
>
> Bison meat was never packed on a running horse, not even blood, as it was believed that doing so would destroy the animal's wind and endurance.
>
> A horse was able to pack the meat of one bison but this was a heavy load. If camp was far off, the flesh of one bison was shared between two pack-horses.[22]

Much care went into guarding the camp. The men served as guards at night while during the day, the young men took out the horses to graze and water. While on the east side of the mountains, the Kootenais never pitched their camp in a river bottom, where enemies could hide among the willows. Rather, they arranged the camp in a circle out on the open plains. At night if scouts brought word of danger of enemies,

> the camp announcer would warn the young warriors. They would ride around outside the camp circle all night, strung out at 15–20 foot intervals, singing songs. If danger was imminent they would ride in groups of four at intervals. In this way it was immediately evident if an enemy attempted to join them in darkness. Each would also tie a half hitch in tail of his horse as additional identification. Anyone detected on foot at night was immediately suspected as an enemy. All the horses were driven inside the camp circle and kept there all night.
>
> If anything suspicious was seen inside [the] camp circle, word was quietly passed to rear and armed guard circle until it reached the originator. The guards would stop singing at once. They would then fire at suspicious object but enemy would usually be gone by this time, warned by the halt in the singing. Sometimes the moon shining on his gun barrel would give him away.[23]

On their meat-laden return trip back across the mountains, the people enjoyed finding the serviceberries ripe and ready for picking. Scouts traveled ahead. They might leave a sign at a fork in the trail—a stick placed in the ground with a small bunch of grass tied to the end. "The angle at which the stick pointed indicated the particular camp site at which the party would stop. . . . If the party was returning in a short time (few days), the tip end of a small fir tree was broken off and placed near the stick."[24]

Kuku Sq̓umu (July), or "Serviceberry Time"

Also known as "Moon of the Red Blooming Lilies"

Summer camps were located around places where serviceberry bushes were abundant. Women and children gathered lots of this important food in July and early August. These were usually dried in the sun and stored away. Sometimes women pounded them in coiled baskets traded from the Lower Kootenais. Such receptacles were preferred to hide or bark containers because the berries stuck to the coiled side of the basket. An unmarked, round stone was used as a pounder. The mashed berries were then molded into cakes, dried in the sun, and stored in parfleches for use as winter traveling food or for food in leaner times.

While the women processed the berries, some people might take the opportunity to go on a journey to acquire paint. Various colors of paints acquired from mineral deposits that were used by the Kootenais included red, green, yellow, and black. One mineral source of red paint was found in what is today Glacier Park. To make the paint, the ochre would be crushed, then mixed with fish oil or animal fat. Another important place to obtain red paint, the most commonly used and valued by all the tribes of the region, was at a place on the Missouri River known in U.S. history as Meriwether Lewis's "Crimson Bluff." Located just south of today's Canyon Ferry Reservoir, the site saw intensive use for at least twelve thousand years, as rich archaeological collections from the area testify.[25]

Plant parts, as well as minerals, provided dyes for paints. Oregon grape roots provided a yellow dye. According to Liz Gravelle, a beautiful turquoise dye could be made from duck droppings.[26] Such materials were used to dye porcupine quills, to dye roots to create patterns in baskets, and to decorate parfleche bags.

In summer camp, women would visit while processing berries, men would talk of their hunting exploits while they repaired tools, and children

Oregon grape Jacqueline Moore, artist

How a Young Brave Survived

▸ ▸ ▸ ▸ ▸ ▸ ▸ ◈ ◂ ◂ ◂ ◂ ◂ ◂ ◂

ONE of the Kootenais' traditional stories demonstrates the importance of learning life skills at an early age.

A young man had somehow been left behind when his people returned home from a buffalo hunt, and he had to survive a winter on his own. He knew how to make essential tools, how to make a fire, how to find and prepare food. His biggest challenges were how to stay warm and how to get enough food. He figured out that he could get both food and a warm robe from a sleeping bear. He found a den and, using a spear he had made, he cautiously poked the darkness that was the den. If there was a bear in the den and the growl sounded hollow, he knew it would be a grizzly den. If it sounded solid it would be a black bear's den. He crawled in and killed the bear, then pulled it out of the cave. He gutted it and dragged it home.

That was one smart and capable boy! He survived the winter and returned home to tell of his exploits.

—Adapted from Mathias, *How a Young Brave Survived*

would play games. Specific games were associated with different seasons. Games, along with chores, taught children the skills they needed to be successful at life.

One game was played by boys who had just returned from the summer buffalo hunt, during the time when the serviceberries were ripe. "Some boys would divide into sides, and were mounted. Long stems of grass were obtained, in the end of which a thorn was placed, to form a dart. They would ride toward each other throwing these, some of which would lodge in the boy's flesh. Whoever cried first was the side that lost."[27]

Another game played during the summer was remembered by Mrs. Tom and told to Claude Schaeffer in 1935:

> Boys and girls join hands and form a circle, with one child inside it. They then move sideways so as to revolve [around] the circle and stop. All lower their hands to the ground, saying, "This is bad place," and then raising them fully erect, upward, saying, "This a good place." The one in the center tries to break through the circle. If she succeeds, all chase her and if caught, the children all rub her head very vigorously. This game was played anytime during the summer, both east and west of the mountains.[28]

Moose, with their antlers covered in velvet, are fat and in the best condition at serviceberry time. The meat is still good before the males go into the rutting season, when they lose weight rapidly. Moose are difficult to hunt, but the Kootenais valued the meat, and moose were plentiful in the swampy, willow-rich areas of the North Fork. When the first moose was killed in summer, a simple, first-foods feast was held. Women prepared the best parts of the animal—the nose, tongue, heart, and the flanks—in a stew for the hunters, then they took the remaining meat for themselves. Even the fleshy outer layer of the antlers, roasted over coals, was eaten.

Bull moose in Glacier Glacier National Park, HPF8332

Caribou and bighorn sheep were also hunted in summer. One method of capturing bighorns involved driving the rams into heavy timber where their horns would get entangled in undergrowth, and hunters could use a knife to kill them. Hunters also watched for the animals to come and lick the salty minerals. Kootenai Mountain and the Kootenai Lick on the east side of Glacier were named by James Willard Schultz after observing Kootenai sheep hunters. According to Schultz, "Some members of the tribe were encamped beside me at the foot of the upper lake. I noticed often that they would ride out of camp at daylight and return at noon or a little later with all the bighorn or goat meat that their horses could carry."[29]

When Schultz asked where these Kootenai hunters went to make their killings so quickly, one of them offered to show him the next day. They rode partway up the Red Eagle Valley and walked to a place where they could look down into a coulee, where they saw a dozen or more bighorns "eating salty clay and drinking from a salt spring that oozes from the ground there." Schultz named the place "Kootenai Lick." The salt licks on the west side of Marias Pass were no doubt one of the places where Kootenai hunters could count on finding bighorns as well as mountain goats.[30]

Once the waters began to recede and the main rivers cleared up, fishing for trout and whitefish resumed. The North Fork of the Flathead was one of the good sites for basket-trap fishing for whitefish.

Baptiste Mathias told Carling Malouf that the area around Hungry Horse, before the dam inundated much of the area, served as a permanent, year-round Kootenai living site where hunters were based. He told of another of these sites near Coram.[31]

Kootenai chief Baptiste Mathias, 1933 Glacier National Park, HPF 5026

Kɛiɬmitiɬq̓ɬikwa'it (August), or
"Berries Ripening during the Night"

Also known as "Moon of the Drying Grass"

Many fruits were gathered during late summer and eaten fresh, including Oregon grape, raspberries, thimbleberries, gooseberries, huckleberries, willow berries, silverberries, rose hips, and buffaloberries. Red currants were boiled and eaten. Oregon grape, elderberries, and the fruit of the hawthorne were dried for future use.

Huckleberry Jacqueline Moore, artist

Most important of all were the huckleberries. Kootenais used to burn out lodgepoles to give the berries more sun and to stimulate growth of new huckleberry bushes. Since old bushes get woody and produce few berries, the best berries are found on young plants.

In late summer, large groups moved to huckleberry grounds in the mountains. Women and children picked while men hunted and fished. Children snared birds and small animals. Women and girls would fill their funnel-shaped berry baskets and preserve much of the fruit for winter use. They would spread the berries out on a flat rock and let the sun dry them.

People still look forward to the huckleberry season and the social life of this season, although the quantities of berries have been greatly reduced. Two women today say that together they can collect only half what their mother alone used to gather in the same area. The active relationship of the people to the berries has diminished, and as a result, the berries are not as prolific.

Buffaloberries ripen in mid-August. Kootenai women would spread hides under the bushes and then thrash them with a stick, knocking the berries onto the hides. Their Kootenai name means "thrash-berry" because of this technique for harvesting. These berries could be eaten fresh or could be sun dried for future use. Buffaloberries are also known as "foamberries," or "Indian ice cream," because, for a treat, these berries, with a little water and sweetener, could be beaten like egg whites to form a frothy treat. Kootenai women used an ingenious little whisk made of bear grass to beat the mixture.

Summer was also a time for acquiring medicines to be dried and stored for the winter. Lovage, a member of the parsley family, was used as an important curative. These roots were gathered in late summer along moist streams in high mountains. The dried roots can be chewed to relieve sore throats and colds. A tea can be made from the roots as well. This root also relieved toothaches, headaches, stomachaches, fevers, and heart

Lovage Jacqueline Moore, artist

problems. And today, dried lovage root remains a common cure among the Kootenais.

As in the past, people still need to know their plants. Naida Lefthand explains that there are two kinds of lovage.[32] The roots smell the same, but the leaves are different. One is an important curative and the other is poisonous.

After seasonal foods were depleted from the lower mountain valleys, the people were ready to cross the mountains, once again, for buffalo. The main purpose of this late summer hunt was to secure summer hides for lodge covers.

The late summer hunt, like the spring hunt, was a post-horse phenomenon and, also like the spring hunt, the Kootenais were often joined by other neighboring tribes. The man chosen to lead the hunt traveled with scouts ahead of the main body of travelers, providing his skill in watching for enemies and other dangers. Another group stayed in the rear. Whereas today Glacier Park sends out trail crews to clear the way, the Kootenais let the animals clear their trails and then the people followed. Trails changed as trees came down; first the animals and then the people went around the deadfall, wherever possible. If a large downfall precluded travel, the people would place burning embers on either side of the log and encourage the coals to burn their way through the log.[33]

In 1858, trader and U.S. government agent William Hamilton and a companion traveled with the Kootenais, who, after a fight with a group of Blackfeet, were attempting to reach the safety of their own territory west of the divide. Hamilton traveled with an advance guard of about fifty Kootenai warriors. This Kootenai group transported their dead and wounded by travois, moving as quickly as possible. Travois are not well suited to the mountains because of their tendency to tip on sloping trails, but, apparently, this was the strategy used to keep the camp moving and to take care of their dead and wounded. Despite their desire to get across the mountains as quickly as possible, knowing that the Blackfeet would return, these Kootenais were unable to travel quickly with their burden.

The Kootenai chief's son, Young Black Bear, the travel leader, knew of a good camp ahead, with water, grass, and wood, where they could bury the dead. They determined to stop there, despite the fact that they weren't yet over the mountains. When they arrived at this camp, every person helped with unpacking and setting up lodges, except about twenty young men who stood sentry on surrounding knolls.

The leaders held council and decided to send two runners ahead to find reinforcements. They then discussed whether they should wait for the reinforcements while staying in this somewhat dangerous location or should attempt to get across the mountains the following day. Chief Black Bear knew that signals were already being transmitted for Blackfeet reinforcements. He was aware that their enemy knew of the pass they were approaching and the places along the trail suitable for camping, and he estimated that by the night of the following day, the Blackfeet would have mobilized five hundred to six hundred warriors.

Just before the Kootenais reached the top of the Continental Divide, about two hundred Blackfeet warriors were upon them. Young Black Bear signaled to those in the rear to close up, and, in moments, the moving village was in a compact circle. The Kootenai warriors stripped to their breech clouts and prepared to die in the defense of their women and children, who were placed on the far side of the pack animals, away from the attackers. The men fought bravely and were able to ward off their attackers long enough for the party to cross the divide and head for home.[34]

Thankfully, most hunting trips were not as difficult as the one remembered from 1858. Usually, the Kootenais would be gone about a month for the summer hunt. Each hunter would return with two or three packhorses loaded down with dried buffalo meat, stored in parfleches. Of course, evenings were full of gambling, storytelling, and fun. This return trip to the west side was traveled at a leisurely pace, with men hunting elk and deer and women gathering berries as they went. This was a season of plenty.

Ku'ɫmakaku (September), or "Ripening of Chokecherries"

Also known as "Moon When Deer Paw Earth"
and "When Antlers Drop Off"

September was the time when chokecherries ripened. Unlike serviceberries and huckleberries, chokecherries have a pit, which required grinding before they were dried and stored. A pestle was used to crush the berries on a stone slab, and then the pulp was formed into cakes and dried. Another method was to take the pulp and spread it out on a small, moist reed mat, work it into the mat to reduce the moisture, and then leave the mat of mashed chokecherries in the sun to dry.[35] Both chokecherries and black hawthorne berries are difficult to eat when mashed and dried.

Drying chokecherries Glenbow Museum, Calgary, Alberta, Canada, NA-5213-29

To remedy the situation, the Kootenais enjoyed them mixed with tallow from the black bear.

Another favorite September food for the Kootenais were the roasted seeds from the cones of the whitebark pine. These pea-sized, nutritious seeds are also highly sought after by some animals. Clark's nutcrackers bury many caches each year in small piles about an inch under the soil, returning to retrieve them the following year. Squirrels gather large stockpiles in underground burrows, fallen logs, and tree cavities to ensure a winter food supply. Taking advantage of these storehouses, rodents and grizzly and black bears will raid the midden piles for their own food resources.

Claude Schaeffer was told that elk season began when the choke-cherries were ripe. Before the rutting season began and while the women gathered and dried berries, hunters focused on elk. They knew the right time by the taste of the stamen from an Indian paintbrush. When it was sweet to the taste, the elk were in prime condition. The Upper Kootenais then moved eastward, into the foothills, for about a month. At this time, the elk have moved to the high country, following good grass along the edge of the timber. One group hunting strategy was for drivers to flush the elk down runways along trails where hunters were waiting. The hunting party tried to kill the lead cow in order to leave the others disoriented and leaderless.

Mrs. Martin of the Tobacco Plains Band described the process of making lodge covers in late summer. She explained that seven or eight women were invited to help make the lodge cover, and the hosting woman served a feast of animal tongues to her volunteers. Following the feast, the elk skins were spread out on the ground in the shape of a lodge. Each woman would have arrived with her own sinew thread and would paint her bundle of sinew red. The next day, the women painted their faces and their dresses with red paint. The leader of the women then fitted and cut the hides to form the lodge cover, and the women started sewing, working from the upper portion downwards on the cover until it was completed.[36]

Bighorns were hunted in their mountain habitat, then hunters moved to higher elevations to get mountain goats, whose coats are best this time

Bighorn ram in Glacier's Swiftcurrent Valley Glacier National Park, HPF 8531

of year. Glacier and Waterton are known for their mountain goats and bighorns, and Upper Kootenai bands commonly hunted them there.

In early September 1885, George Bird Grinnell and his small party camped between the St. Mary Lakes. They encountered a Kootenai man traveling on horseback from his camp several miles down the St. Mary River. The last official buffalo hunt had been in 1880, but this did not stop Kootenais from coming across the divide into the east side of what is now Glacier Park to hunt and trap. That year, Kootenais managed to acquire forty-four sheep, a few elk, a black bear, a grizzly, and a moose. They were hunting west of the junction of the St. Mary Lakes, in the area of Singleshot Mountain. (The naming of this mountain is associated with this 1885 trip and a lucky shot by Grinnell himself.) Knowing that the previous winter (1883–1884) was known as "Starvation Winter" among the Blackfeet, it is remarkable that any game remained in these mountains. With the demise of the buffalo just a year or two previously, the Blackfeet had put intense hunting pressure on the eastern slope of the mountains. Given the general dearth of game, the ample harvest of sheep and other animals is a testament to the skills of the Kootenai hunters.

Grinnell commented on the impressive mountain hunting skills of these Kootenai hunters. After a fierce rainstorm, followed by snow and fog that forced the hunters off the mountain, Grinnell and his party of two Pikunni men went back up Singleshot Mountain the following day with two Kootenai guides. Grinnell couldn't keep up with the Kootenai mountaineers. He had to stop to rest and catch his breath. He called to them and, with sign language, tried to make them understand that he wanted them to slow down, but he lost sight of them as they disappeared into the fog.[37]

In addition to hunting, acquiring furs was another early fall activity. Joe Dennis told Claude Schaeffer about beaver trapping on the North Fork:

> Andrew Bear Hat used a hide canoe for several weeks in beaver trapping along the North Fork of Flathead in early fall. We would stake out the traps along the shore from his canoe and thus avoid the deep snow on the banks and also avoid leaving a scent. He made the canoe upon reaching the river and would throw the carcass in the canoe. He would live on the beaver flesh and also dry it.

Dennis remembered that, when he was a boy of twelve, "a good muzzle-loader, flint-lock gun was worth of 12 beaver."[38]

Beaver at work Glacier National Park, HPF 4042

Although people were busy gathering and processing foods for the winter, life was good and there was always time for fun. David Thompson was frustrated by the Kootenais' lack of interest in helping to supply the traders' camp with meat, complaining that they spent more time gambling than hunting.[39] (This frustration might reveal more about David Thompson and European values than about the Kootenais.)

K̓upaqułaqpi'k (October), or "Autumn Leaves Fade and Fall"

As snow was beginning to accumulate in the high country, family groups came down from berry gathering and hunting there and spread out along various trails, hunting elk and deer in the lower mountains of what today are Glacier and Waterton and similar environments within their territory.

The North Fork was one of the most important places in the fall, with its vast meadows, forests, and streams that provided food for elk, deer, and moose. The Kootenais employed several methods for killing "four-leggeds" during the fall. The common approach was for men to be "stationed along runways while others above them drive deer and elk down to lower levels." As told to Paul Baker:

> A hunting expedition for deer, moose, elk, or buffalo was set up in the same way. It was called "drive-hunting." Everyone went on the hunt. A place was found where the animals could be driven into a narrow place such as between two hills or mountains. Sometimes it was necessary to erect a barricade between the mountains. The men who were more active would go out a distance and start the animals toward the barricade. The children, older men, and women would be stationed in such a way as to herd the animals into the proper enclosure. Men had been appointed to do the killing when the animals got to the barricade. The women and children, with the use of sharp rocks, skinned the animals, prepared the flesh and hides for use.[40]

During the rutting season, solitary bull elk were brought within shooting range by means of a call made from a stalk of wild rhubarb. Elk hides were preferred over the hides of buffalo for making robes and tipi covers since the elk hides are easier to tan and are very durable.

Fall was the best time to acquire goat hides from which to make robes. People would go into the mountains and hope to return to their camp

Hunting with Dogs

▶ ▶ ▶ ▶ ▶ ▶ ▶ ◈ ◀ ◀ ◀ ◀ ◀ ◀ ◀

THE Tobacco Plains people also used dogs to drive the deer. One elder told Claude Schaeffer about a time when the usual method wasn't working:

> [A] leader with strong power volunteered to try another [method]. . . . The hunters, armed with guns, started out in a body and dropped aside, one by one, but [stayed] within sight of each other until they formed a long line. The end man, who was the leader, then gave the howl of a wolf, and the man beside him a whistle which was carried along the line of men to the first who also gave the wolf howl, at which the line was set in motion. The hunters advanced in this way through the brush and in but a short time had killed sufficient deer to load a packhorse. In the beginning most of the men had doubted that such a drive would be successful, since the dogs were free to run ahead and frighten the game.

—Excerpted from the Schaeffer Papers

laden with material for winter robes. When you tan a goat with the hair on, it's much softer than a buffalo robe. Buffalo robes would be good for a floor covering, but the goat hide made a soft bed.

The creeks ran with many varieties of fish at this time of year. Even though fall was important for hunting four-legged animals, fishing brought in another source of protein. Jerome Hewankorn called this

Mountain goats Danny On, photographer, Glacier National Park, HPF 9089

Kootenai encampment with a fish trap lying in the foreground, Tobacco Plains, 1861 Library of Congress, LC-USZC4-11437

"whitefish season." Whitefish, highly valued for its good flavor, somewhat like halibut, was readily available at this time of year. Enjoyed fresh, this fish was also dried for winter stores.

Fall was also the season when the tobacco leaves were ready to harvest. These were gathered and sun dried or dried on a rock at the edge of a fire. Everyone got a share, and enough tobacco was grown to last throughout the year. However, the Kootenais quit growing tobacco after Cree traders introduced commercial tobacco to them in the early eighteenth century.

The stalks of dogbane, known as "Indian hemp," were harvested in the fall along creeks and other moist areas below five thousand feet. The Kootenais used the silky fiber from the bark to make twine and ropes and even to sew tule mats together for tipi covers. Hemp processing was very involved. Women gathered the stalks after the leaves had dropped, then split them and scraped away the bark and pith with a sharp piece of wood. They wrapped these processed stalks into bundles, which they kept for a year. The next year, these fibers were plaited into ropes. After drying in the sun, the strands were unbraided and dried even more. These processed

Dogbane, also known as Indian hemp
Jacqueline Moore, artist

fibers were finally ready to be made into rope. Every woman carried a ball of thread for sewing.

Elk hunting ended right after the rutting season, when the elk lose weight and "become poor." Hunters then headed back across the mountains for the fall buffalo hunt. This trip had to be carefully timed since horses provided the transportation. Passes such as Crowsnest and Marias, both significantly lower than Logan, were used. When it was time for the buffalo hunt, the scouts would establish a place across the Rockies, in advance, for the various families to meet up. Claude Schaeffer was told by Mrs. Pascal that they would plan to be on the east side in October when the buffalo "started to move into forested areas to escape cold weather." "The Akanahonek [Tobacco Plains Band] would wait for each other on the last bench of the Rockies, meanwhile hunting goat, sheep and elk, until all the parties had arrived. The last were larger families which hunted mountain game. The Akanahonek moved to Waterton Lakes and then south to St. Mary's Lake, where they hunted elk, deer, moose, sheep and goat. They travelled with horses and sometimes they would go far out on the plains. This was after peace [was] made with [the] Blackfoot."[41]

The late October hunt took advantage of buffalo moving into the foothills for shelter from early winter storms. Before the Upper Kootenais acquired horses, they used their game-driving skills to run buffalo over steep cliffs. Once horses were incorporated into their lifeway, it was easier to ride into a group of grazing buffalo than to conduct all the preparations needed for establishing and using a drive site. A good horse could be ridden right into the midst of a herd where the hunter could dispatch several animals before the others would spook and run.

When Hamilton and McKay encountered the Kootenais in the mountains in the fall of 1858, they were wearing heavy caribou moccasins, which the traders admired. They asked to have some made and soon were provided with six pairs. Hamilton doesn't say whether the women traveled with caribou hide, but given the timeframe and location, they must have traveled with the material to supply the travelers' needs. In the century before these mountains became Glacier National Park, mountain caribou was a common animal in Kootenai territory.

Kootenai hunters took advantage of whatever meat they could bring in this time of year, as noted by David Thompson in October 1806. While at Kootenae House on Lake Windemere, he observed that trout, swans, elk, and deer were widely available and that Kootenai hunters like False

Mountain caribou Danny On, photographer, Glacier National Park, HPF 5326

Dog (Chien Faux) and Left Hand (The Gauche) brought in meat on a regular basis.

Everyone carried their particular tool kit, anticipating all of the activities they might engage in during the journey. In addition to hunting, they were also prepared for spearing bull trout along the North Fork of the Flathead and at key places on the South Fork. These large fish were speared with a detachable, single-prong fish spear made of a goat's horn. The fishing was limited to one day when conditions were just right. Several men would drive the fish toward shallow water where others waited to spear them. As reported by Claude Schaeffer, "This single-prong spear, like the beaver spear, was thrown so as to impale the fish. In its struggles, the fish soon dislodged the barbed head from the shaft, the latter serving

Fall harvest Andrew Campbell, photographer, in Olga Weydemeyer Johnson, *Flathead and Kootenay: The Rivers, the Tribes, and the Regions Traders* (Glendale, Calif.: A.H. Clark Co., 1969), 67

as a drag to tire the fish. Most hunters carried such a spear head (made from mountain goat horn), as part of their regular travel equipment."[42] Since the long wooden shaft was awkward to pack, these were made on site when needed. A braided horsehair line held it all together.

On the return trip from east of the divide, before returning to the base camp locations at lower elevations, men again hunted bighorn sheep and mountain goats as needed to ensure a good winter. However, Kootenais were not afraid of the mountains in winter. With snowshoes and bow and arrows, they could venture into the high country to acquire meat if deer and elk became depleted in the vicinity of the winter camp.

Not only did their dried stores provide food for winter, but they also enabled the Kootenais to make their difficult trip back over the mountains for buffalo in February, after the snow had set up. Thinking ahead as they returned west from this fall hunt, they cached meat on platforms in the forks of tall trees that could be recovered and eaten during the next winter buffalo hunt. Clearly, it was important to plan ahead. The people had to be thinking about which routes were both horse- and snowshoe-accessible to make this plan work.

While traveling, they looked for opportunities to trade. In the fall of 1800, David Thompson was impressed by a group of Kootenais, led by four men "of steady demeanor," who visited a Piegan camp on the east side of the mountains. The friendly Pikunni chief invited them to feast, and some of the young men challenged the Kootenais to a gambling match. This time the Kootenais won every game. It wasn't always so.

K̓taⱡuʼk Ȼupqa (November), or "Deer Rutting" or "Deer Calling"

After the fall buffalo-hunting season, depending on the snow line, people regrouped in the lower-elevation prairies. Camps were chosen in close proximity to concentrations of deer. People from the Tobacco Plains Band told Claude Schaeffer that they returned from the fall buffalo hunt in the middle of November. Usually their stores of dried meat were sufficient at this time to require little or no hunting during the winter.

In November 1806, David Thompson was anxious to get the Kootenais trapping more, as beaver and other fur-bearing animals were in their prime for pelts. "But winter was traditionally a time of relative leisure for the Kootenais because game was concentrated in the valleys and the bands could gather together to socialize. In mid-November the families tenting near Kooteneae House were all busy accumulating meat for a big dancing feast."[43]

Depending upon need, a succession of hunts would be conducted at different localities throughout late fall and into winter until enough food had been acquired, bringing the communal hunting season to a close. Every family had to come prepared with food for the annual renewal celebration at what is now Apgar at Lake McDonald.

Winter deer drives required experienced knowledge of snow conditions. Claude Schaeffer was told that the winter deer-hunting group would locate the wintering areas of the deer and then select a narrow valley leading off from this area for the drive. The hunt leader would call for volunteers to serve as drivers and bowmen. The drivers, also known as "shouters," would line up at the lower end of the valley, and, when signaled by the leader, would start forward, flushing out the game:

> Each one shouted, *hu! hu!* as he advanced, both to keep even with his neighbors on each side, and also to startle the deer. The leader moves forward usually in advance of the beaters, or if the latter are too few, at one end of the line. The deer, now forced to abandon the areas in which they have kept the snow beaten down, . . . flounder through the deep drifts up the valley. The drivers continue to press upon their flanks while a few hunters stationed along the sides prevent any animal from doubling back and escaping. Those animals that take to the available runways are killed as they pass by hunters stationed nearby.
>
> Some of the hunters were stationed in a line across the upper end of the valley where they could intercept the deer, while others stood beside the runways. The hunters were referred to as "people sheltered under trees."
>
> Warned by the approaching noise of the drivers that the game is close at hand, the row of bowmen now hold themselves in readiness. The fleeing animals are allowed to approach quite closely before any arrows are discharged, so that they will not attempt to turn back. If possible, they attempt to kill the leader of the herd first and thus temporarily demoralize the animals. By the time the beaters have come up, those deer that have not escaped have been slain.[44]

Group cooperation was emphasized for deer drives. A leader made sure that no one left camp to hunt alone. After a successful hunt, the leader was responsible for distributing equal shares to all families in the camp. Men stopped hunting for a few days in order to give the women

Mule deer at Lake McDonald R. E. "Ted" Marble, photographer, Glacier National Park, HPF 8020

adequate time to prepare and dry the meat and work the hides. These thick wintertime hides were put to good use as moccasins and other items requiring this added durability.

K̓usmukusaɬ Ȼxamaɬiɬ (December), or "First Prayers"

Also known as "Moon When Wolves Run Together," "Moon When Deer Shed Antlers," and, in Canada, "The Sun Goes Under" (Nistamu)

With ample stores of food on hand, and much of the dried meat stored in log caches where it would remain until March, the long nights of winter provided time for the community to hear, once again, the stories of the people, passed down generation after generation, since time immemorial.

Coyote is a central character in many of the Kootenai stories.[45] His antics helped Kootenais learn about their own characteristics, both strengths and weaknesses, and the stories helped them to learn about appropriate behavior. In the quiet nights of winter, the crackling fire might be the only sound other than the animated voice of the storyteller.

Regular chores continued during the daylight hours. Children played games in the snow and helped bring in firewood and water. Everything and everybody slowed down and rested during this season. Women continued to make sure that a good supply of winter clothing and moccasins was available. Men repaired tools and talked of significant things that had happened since the last winter.

As the nights grew longer, people readied themselves for the winter renewal ceremony at the foot of Lake McDonald, grateful to have survived another year. They had circled through the seasons once again and joyfully gathered together in their original place to dance and sing the songs taught to them by the spirits at the beginning of time.

Next time you're at Apgar, pause and remember. If you're quiet enough and willing enough, maybe you'll hear a song.

Chapter 6

◈

The Pikunni Worldview

BY THE PIKUNNI TRADITIONAL ASSOCIATION

Learning from our Ancestors

BETTY Bastien of the Siksika (the northernmost Blackfoot band) writes beautifully of the world in which we were raised in her book *Blackfoot Ways of Knowing*. She explains how relating to the natural forces with respect is the fundamental premise of our ethical and moral conduct. Striving to maintain balance is respectful of "the natural order of the cosmic universe." This law influences the way we understand our surroundings, relate to each other, and organize ourselves socially. Our medicine pipes and bundles contain the collective teachings and provide structure and guidance for the way we conduct ourselves in relation to each other and the natural world.[1]

Key elements in our identity include our relationship to our home-land, the territory originally given to us by the Creator and where we still remain; our bundles; the way we pitch our lodges and the way we design and paint them; our straight-up war bonnets; our black-stone pipes; and the Okan Medicine Lodge. To understand our way of life, people must have some introduction to the spiritual practices that guide us through the seasons. We share these with you here in the hope of greater understanding of one another and of all life in this land we share.

The Ancient Ones tell us how the world was made and how the Black-feet people came about. From these oral traditions comes our Genesis.

In the Beginning

▶ ▶ ▶ ▶ ▶ ▶ ▶   ◈   ◀ ◀ ◀ ◀ ◀ ◀ ◀

IN the beginning the Creator (Ista-pay-ta-bee-yope-ah) made the Sun (Natosi). The Creator was lonely in this great dark hollow of space. Creator thought he would make some small balls of dirt to play with, and so he made the planets circle around him and the Sun. He soon chose Earth to be his favorite. He surrounded her with air, and Sun would keep her warm so all future things would grow on Earth.

Creator made himself small so that he could play on Earth. He made a snake as his first playmate. Soon there were so many snakes they became very disrespectful. Creator then made Earth so hot that all snakes died except one female. This one female was left so that in later years there would still be snakes.

Creator noticed that Earth was bare of nice things so he created the green grasses and flowers. And again he thought he should create something in his image to play games with while he was on Earth. He created the Moon (Ko-ko-mi-ki-soom) and blew air in its nostrils and gave her life. The Moon would provide the Creator with many children. Moon would be the Creator's first wife and the Earth his second wife.

Creator also made Napi, First Old Man (Om-muck-kin-nah), to be his human helper. Napi was given special powers to help him accomplish his deeds while roaming the Earth.

In those early days, Humans and Star people lived on Earth together. Soon Humans became jealous of the Star people. When Human children killed a Star child, Star people moved into the sky. The Star people convinced the Creator to flood the earth to kill off Humans. Creator made the rains for many days. Finally, Napi and a few animals were stranded on a mountaintop, which we know now as Chief Mountain, where Napi made the rainbow, Napi's Rope (Naapi-wa-oto-katsis), and roped the clouds to make it stop raining.

Napi asked the animals to dive into the water and retrieve him some mud. The first animal to try, but fail, was the duck. Many other animals tried but failed. Last to try was the muskrat. Muskrat was gone for a long time, finally surfacing with a fistful of mud. That is why muskrats have paws like Humans. Napi used the mud to make the water recede, and life got going again.

—Compiled from oral histories
passed down by our elders

Chief Mountain T. J. Hileman, photographer, Glacier National Park, 5075d

Cutbank Pass trail Yale Collection of Western Americana, Beinecke Rare Book and Manuscript Library, Yale University, New Haven, Connecticut, 1098739

Objects on Earth such as animals, plants, rocks, and the Earth herself, we call them "Earth Beings" (Ksah-komi-tapiksi). Back in those days, animals could talk to Humans. Even rocks and trees could talk. All living things could communicate with each other. Animals could take Human forms so they could share their special gifts with Humans, creating "Transferred Rights."[2]

In addition to Earth Beings (Ksah-komi-tapiksi), which include both Human Beings and Other Than Human Beings (Naahks), there are the Above Beings (Spo-mi-tapisksi) and the Water Beings (Soo-yi-tapiksi). The Above Beings include Natosi, the Sun; his wife, Ko-ko-mi-ki-soom, the Moon; and their son, Ipiso-waahsa; the Morning Star, along with other stars, and also Thunder; the Sky and spirits of the sky; and many birds. The Water Beings include Cold Maker and his helper, Wind Maker; water birds; and beavers, muskrats, otters, and other animals that live in and near the water, along with the Soo-yi-tapi, spirits of the water.

The land that is now Glacier National Park is the home to some of the most important Beings. Thunder, whose home is Chief Mountain (located at the northeast corner of the park), is a source of some of the sacred Medicine Pipe bundles. Wind Maker lives in a high mountain lake and, by stirring up the water, creates the wind. While Walter McClintock and his Pikunni guide, Siksikai-koan, were camping near the Continental Divide along the Cutbank trail in 1896, Siksikai-koan told McClintock about Wind Maker: "Long ago an Indian, who camped in this valley, saw the Wind Maker rise from the waters of a lake. He was like a monster bull elk. When he flapped his ears, the wind blew hard; and when he sank again beneath the water, the wind went down.[3]

Underwater Beings also inhabit a cave at the base of Running Eagle (Pitamakan) Falls in Glacier, above Lower Two Medicine Lake. It is well known that that hole in the cliff from which the river gushed is inhabited by Underwater People. From our first fathers, the tale has come down to us that, in the beginning, no cliff was there.

> When Old Man made the world, he made a straight, smooth, deep valley there, beginning it at the summit of the mountains and extending it out across the plains. He had, of course, first made the mountains. But he was sometimes careless in his work. Just here, to the right of the valley, he had made a high, slender mountain and failed to set it straight up; it leaned to the south; and after he had made the valley it toppled over, forming this rock wall across it. Above, among the big loose rocks that filled the valley, the river sank out of sight, only to reappear gushing from the dark hole in the wall. When Old Man returned to this place and saw what had happened, he blamed himself. Said he, "I should have been more careful. If I had set that mountain straight up like the others it would not have fallen. In my haste I only made more work for myself. I have now to clear the valley of this great mass of rock that fills it."
>
> But just then he saw that the fallen mountain had not stopped the flow of the river, saw its waters gushing from the strange, dark hole in the wall rock. "Ha! It is best that I leave this falling just as it is," he said. "That hole in there, and the deep pool below, will be a good home for some of my Underwater People." And with that he turned about and went off to other of his world-making work.[4]

And the Old Man made vegetation to sprout from the earth, roots and leaves from plants for his people to eat and juices from these plants. And he made the animals to give Human Beings meat to eat. And with these came certain rules, which foods to eat and how to use the plants and animals they harvested. Even today, bundle holders follow these rules of acceptable foods. Other people had to forego these ancient rules when faced with starvation. One band is called Fish-Eaters to mark the change in the Creator's proscription against eating his Underwater Beings. But bundle holders have remained faithful; they can't handle or consume certain animals and birds represented in their bundles. So, although some

Running Eagle Falls Glacier National Park, 11719

How Food Came to the People

THE first people ate only vegetation—the roots and leaves from the plants, the berries, and the different kinds of bark, also the juices from these plants—because there wasn't any kind of meat to use as food. As the number of people increased, Creator Sun saw that they were hungry. He told them that he would make more reliable and filling food for them, and he did. He took mud and fashioned the first buffalo, then a second, to be food for the people.

Time passed before Creator Sun came back for a visit. When he did, he found that once again, the population had grown so much that people didn't have enough food to eat. He found Mudman, his first human creation, and they sat together by a stream to talk of how to care for the people. As they made themselves comfortable on the ground, Creator Sun dug into the mud along the water's edge. He molded this mud into another of his creatures with four legs with split hooves like the buffalo. Creator Sun told [Mudman], "These creatures that I'm now making for you and all of the children to use as food, they shall all have split feet."

That creature was a bit smaller than the buffalo. Creator Sun told Mudman, "We will know this one by its feet and legs. You will see why when you see this one run in the fields or forests and mountains, through the heavy growth of trees. I'll name it *biikbeek-si-gow.*" The name the Creator gave this animal, which we today know as the elk, means magic feet and legs. Creator Sun took more mud from the brook's edge and molded a smaller animal than the elk. He told Mudman, "We shall know this one from how it throws its legs . . . *aw-wake-ausi.* . . . This one too shall roam anywhere, be it the plains, the timber, the mountains, or the foothills. It will be just as sure-footed as the elk and fast for its own survival." These are today's whitetail deer.

Many more creatures were made from mud at the water's edge. To bring them to life, Creator Sun would blow into their nostrils. Of each kind, he made both a male and a female. He made a second kind of deer, known as *es-si-go-do-yi,* or the blacktail. And he molded the bighorn mountain sheep, taking a bone from it to make a female to bear little ones to increase as time went along. This one was to be known as the *oo-ma-kiki-ni,* or big head. "This animal will be of the mountains," Creator Sun said.

And Creator Sun made more animals—the moose and the antelope. All of the food animals were made and given to Mudman. He was given a lesson in how to stalk them, how to kill them, and how to dress all of them out. He was taught how to cook them and how to preserve them for later use. How to preserve the hides for use as clothing and shelter. The smaller animals were for clothing mostly and the larger ones for shelter, but all of them were for food. Mudman was taught not to waste any of the animals, even the bones were to be used for something.

After creating all of these animals for food for the people, Creator Sun had to return to the sky. Later, there were so many of these split hooves that Creator Sun had to make carnivores to help eat them. In addition to four-legged animals, there were also two categories of birds created—"all birds that fly" and "beings running on the ground"—and these are also acceptable foods, except for restrictions for bundle holders. Fish were not to be eaten. These, and other animals of the water, were to be food for the Soo-yi-tapiksi, the Underwater Spirits.[5]

—Adapted from Bullchild, *Sun Came Down,* 54–61

people eat ducks and geese, for example, this is restricted food for those with these birds represented in their bundle. Thunder Pipe holders won't sleep on pillows of duck feathers and won't bring rabbit fur or bear skins into their lodges. They don't even speak the name of "bear" aloud.

Since the beginning of time, our ancestors studied the habits of birds and animals and observed their warnings. Our ancestors understood the character of the different moons, and they looked to the sky for clues about the weather. Our bundle holders continue these practices today in order to take care of the people.

Bundles and Ceremonies

The Blackfeet world is defined by a sequence of ceremonies, bundle openings, and the Medicine Lodge, the Okan. Some call this the Sun Dance, but it should not be confused with the Sun Dance of the Lakota and other tribes. The Okan is a ceremony uniquely our own, brought down from the stars by Scarface, the son of Feather Woman and Morning Star.

Since long before the horse came to the people, we have had bundles. These are teachings from other Beings who transfer their powers to us. We

Beaver Bundle of Mad Wolf (at the foot of the tripod), 1903 Walter McClintock, photographer, Yale Collection of Western Americana, Beinecke Rare Book and Manuscript Library, Yale University, New Haven, Connecticut, 1098059

St. Mary Lake and Wild Goose Island T. J. Hileman, photographer, Glacier National Park, 3190

have bundles given by the Beaver and others that are gifts from Thunder. Each bundle has unique qualities and came to us in unique circumstances. The bundles contain hides and claws and feathers and teeth and bones from the various animals who share with us. Songs go with each item. The collection of objects is wrapped in a hide. In the old days, the pipe and a second, smaller pipe for that bundle were tied to the outside, but today pipes are included inside the bundle with the other objects.

Each bundle is tended by a man and a woman. The bundle keepers are the traditional community leaders, the wise counselors who collectively make important decisions for the community, always drawing on the spiritual teachings of the bundles.

The Beaver Bundle is the oldest of the Blackfeet bundles. Linda Juneau (Pikunni), in her thesis on the Small Robe Band, tells us that the Beaver Bundle "contents and the specific ritual associated with its opening symbolize human interdependency with all creatures and elements of the environment." The Beaver Bundle has over one hundred songs that "provide the rules for living in harmony with all Creation. The rules tell us how to control ourselves, to limit ourselves. . . . We limit our curiosity. We limit our creation and our creativity because of these rules [of nature]."[6]

Many Beaver Bundles serve the people. The story of one from St. Mary Lakes tells of Apikunni, spending a winter alone on the island now known as Wild Goose Island. There he was befriended and cared for by a family of beavers.[7]

Thunder Pipes also come from the Backbone of the World, in the mountains of Glacier Park. Chief Mountain is the source of the first Thunder Pipe. Two hundred years ago, in 1809, explorer Alexander Henry found himself in a Pikunni camp. There he learned about the history and importance of the Thunder Pipe. Thunder, he was told, was someone who was very wicked and troublesome to the Indians, killing men and beasts in great number. But many years ago he made peace with the Blackfeet and gave them a pipestem in token of his friendship. Since then he has been harmless. This pipestem they still possess; it is taken care of by Three Bulls, one of their chiefs.[8]

The oldest pipe among the South Pikunni was kept by George and Molly Kicking Woman for many years. It originated at Chief Mountain and is thought to be the one described by Edward Curtis as "the greatest of all medicine-bundles, the one containing the long-time pipe, which has been in possession of the tribe for as long as the memory of man can tell. The tribe possesses many other medicine pipes, but this is *the* pipe. Its origin is accounted for in the following myth:

> Heavy clouds hung low over the earth, and thunder rolled. A great storm threatened, causing all the people to be filled with fear. A beautiful girl, the only child of a chief, went out and said, "Thunder, take away the storm and I will marry you!" The thunder ceased, the tumultuous clouds grew quiet and passed away, and the sky cleared. Not long thereafter the girl happened to be alone a short distance from the camp. A man appeared before her and said, "I am the man you promised to marry." The girl, remembering her promise, went with him into the sky. She lived there with

A Beaver Bundle Story

ONE Beaver Bundle story tells of an event that took place at Lower St. Mary Lake, right at the edge of Glacier National Park. Details in this story date it to a time thousands of years ago, before people had dogs to help carry their belongings. James White Calf told this old story to Adolf Hungry Wolf in July 1968, with George and Molly Kicking Woman interpreting:

An old Pikunni chief, a great hunter and trapper, used to travel all over to catch different kinds of birds and animals. He hunted buffalo, elk, bears, and all the other big animals. He made pits and caught eagles. He made deadfalls and trapped all the different kinds of small animals for their furs.

He spent the trapping season camping with his young wife and their small child on the north end of Lower St. Mary Lake, above the place where the highway bridge crosses today.

One day this man went out to check his traps. When he came home that evening, he found his baby son alone and crying, but his wife was nowhere around. He searched, but he couldn't even find her trail. At first he thought she would return later, but with more time he finally decided that a bear must have killed her and carried her away.

That night, a spirit came into the lodge and spoke to him, saying, "Pity you and your poor child. I came to tell you not to worry about your wife; she is alive. She was taken into the lake and is now in the lodge of the Underwater Persons, where she is safe. I'll come again and help you to get her back." Then the spirit left.

The next night, he returned and said to the man: "Here is what you have to do to get your wife back. Hide near the water. Watch for a little white beaver. If you can capture him, you'll get your wife back. That little white beaver is the son of the Beaver Chief. I'll come back again to tell you how to catch this little beaver."

The spirit returned and told the man how to catch the little beaver with his bare hands, warning him to take care not to hurt him. It took a few days, but finally the man saw the little white beaver, heading toward shore. The man managed to catch the young beaver once he was out of the water and took him home to his lodge.

The spirit came for the fourth time and warned the man that "two Underwater Persons will come to ask for the white beaver." The spirit instructed him to stay put, not to leave the little beaver alone, and to prepare a place for the Underwater Persons to sit. Later that night the man heard sounds coming from the lake, so he prepared the seats in his lodge. The Underwater Persons appeared in human form. They found the man sitting at the back of his lodge with both his own baby boy and also the little white beaver on his lap. One of them said, "We have a message from the Beaver Chief. If you send back his son, he will turn your wife free."

The man shook his head and said, "No, I'll just keep him here so my son will have someone to play with until his mother comes back." The Underwater Spirits said they would speak to the Beaver Chief about it. They told him to prepare a place for an altar behind his fireplace. At that time, this man had no medicine articles in his lodge.

The next morning before sunrise, the man got up and fixed his lodge and cleared a space for an altar. Then the two Underwater Persons arrived with an incense fork and some other things. They said that the Beaver Chief was on his way, bringing his wife, and also with many of his followers who were coming to bring gifts. A short time later, the sound of singing voices came from the lake, and the man recognized his wife's voice among them.

Then his wife came in through the door-way first, carrying a strange bundle, which she placed on an empty seat in the back, beside her husband. She took the incense tongs, a forked stick, and placed a coal on the cleared space in order to make incense. Then the Beaver Chief entered, followed by many different water animals, water birds, land animals, and land birds.

They all sat down and sang a song, which they repeated four times.

The Beaver Chief now told the man about the gift brought by the man's wife, explaining that it was the Beaver Chief's "bundle of bags in which I keep my medicines and my tobacco" and that they had come to transfer the bundle to the man. In exchange, the Beaver Chief asked for many items from the man, including eagle tail feathers, the skin of a black coyote, a fisher, and a white buffalo calf, all of which the man had among his trappings and was able to provide.

Then the Beaver Chief said, "Now I have transferred to you my bundle and four of the important things. These I give to you along with your wife. Now give me back my son."

But the man said, "It is not enough. My son and I suffered when you took the woman, so now you must please us. What else will you give us to go with this bundle?"

The Beaver Chief asked the other Under-water Persons to help him out. So the different birds and animals sang their songs and added their medicines to the bundle. Most gave their skins or the feathers. The last ones to contribute were the turtle, the lizard, and the frog. The turtle didn't have a song of his own, but he was wise and borrowed a song from the lizard. Then the frog stood up and said he, too, had no song to sing. The turtle knocked him over backwards, but in falling, the frog held up seven fingers. Nobody knew what that meant, so he told them, "I don't have a song to contribute, but I'll give you seven months for the ceremony to be held."

The man said to the Beaver Chief, "You haven't given me enough. What more can you add to the bundle?" The Beaver Chief said, "I will give you my whistle, which you can blow when the people dance with all these different skins." The elk and the otter said they would also add their whistles. So the man said, "The white buffalo calf has contributed his skin to the bundle, but the rest of the Buffalo People haven't given anything. What can they add to the bundle?' The buffalo cow said, "I'll contribute my hide to wrap the bundle." Then the buffalo bull said, "I'll contribute my hooves." Then the Beaver Chief painted the man's face, and also the face of the man's son, while the wife of the Beaver Chief painted the man's wife. For this, they sang the painting song.

Then the man said, "There is only one more thing that I want, then it will be enough. I need a strong dog with a travois to carry this bundle." The Beaver Chief shook his head sadly and said that that's one thing he didn't have, since he lived under water and didn't need to take the bundle around on land. But then the Spirit Man came in, the one that advised the man how to get his wife back. He said, "I can help you with this." Then he sang a song with these words: "I want a dog to come in with a travois on his back."

Then the Spirit Man said, "I will go up to Water Dog Lake (near St. Mary Lake and Duck Lake) and bring you a dog from there." Soon he was back, leading two dogs, a male and a female. The male dog was hauling a travois. The Spirit Man said, "The male dog will carry your bundle, and I also brought a female dog, so that they can mate and multiply. From now on, they will carry all your belongings whenever you move camp."

This is how we first got our dogs, long ago. And it is said that there are still water dogs in Water Dog Lake.

—Based on Hungry Wolf, *Blackfoot Papers*, 2:482–83

him for a time, then began to long for her father, and Thunder allowed her to return, giving her a pipestem for a present to her father. This was the Long-time Pipe.[9]

George Kicking Woman talked with Adolph Hungry Wolf about this Long-time Pipe and its stories. Some objects within this bundle date back to the dog days, before the people had horses. He told of a long whistle used "to invite all the spirits—all the birds in the bundle, all the animals, the ones running around, the little ones, the deer—all of them." The leaders of the ceremony would say "*Puch-sapooat*," or "Come and dance," because they wanted "to make sure [the spirits] hear us so they will all come to join us in the ceremony."[10]

The Blackfeet referred to the time before the people had horses as the dog days, when dogs pulled the travois. American Museum of Natural History, 31508

"There's some birds in my bundle that are so old and worn out from being danced and prayed with," Kicking Woman explained, "that they've got no heads left on them, or else they're missing legs and wings. There are all kinds of bird skins in there. There are some ducks—we sing a special song for them. And the geese. And also the loon—that's one of the main ones. This is the loon song," Kicking Woman said as he sang a couple of rounds. "And then there's the owl, and it's got a song."[11]

In the summer of 2010, a century after the creation of Glacier National Park and unknown centuries since Thunder told the people how to protect

The Long-Time Pipe

LONG ago, the father of Brings Down the Sun had a vision on Chief Mountain in which he learned of the origin of this important pipe. He was camped with his grandfather and father on the Green Banks River, now called the St. Mary River. His elders were "digging out" beavers, which were very plentiful. His father went out hunting alone, hoping to supply the camp with meat. He followed an elk trail up the side of a steep mountain, then, above timberline, he followed a herd of mountain sheep to Chief Mountain.

When he drew near the summit, he discovered a dense, foul-smelling smoke rising from a deep pit. He pushed a huge boulder into it to hear it fall. There came back no sound, but a cloud of smoke and gas arose so dense and suffocating that he turned to flee, only to meet a black cloud coming up the mountain side. He was frightened and tried to escape, but suddenly there came a terrible crash, and he fell to the ground. He beheld a woman standing over him. Her face was painted black, and there were red zigzag streaks like lightning below her eyes. Behind the woman stood a man holding a large weapon. My father heard the man exclaim impatiently, "I told you to kill him at once, but you stand there pitying him." Then he heard the woman chant, "When it rains, the noise of the Thunder is my medicine."

The man also sang and fired his big weapon. The report was like a deafening crash of thunder, and my father beheld lightning coming from the big hole on the mountain top. He knew nothing more until he found himself lying inside a great cavern. He had no power to speak, neither could he raise his head, but when he heard a voice saying, "This is the person who threw the stone down into your fireplace," he realized that he was in the lodge of the Thunder Maker.

He heard the beating of a drum, and, after the fourth beating, he was able to sit up and look around. The spirit he saw was the Thunder Chief, in the form of a huge bird, with his wife and many children around him. All of the children had drums, painted with the green talons of the Thunder-bird and with Thunder-bird beaks, from which issued zigzag streaks of yellow lightning. (Whenever Isis-a-kummi, or Thunder-bird, leaves his lodge to go through the heavens with the storm clouds, he takes the form of a great bird with many colors, like the rainbow, and with long green claws. The lightning is the trail of the Thunder-bird.)

As Thunder Maker smoked his pipe, he would blow two whiffs upward toward the sky and then two whiffs toward the earth. After each whiff, the thunder crashed. Finally, the Thunder-bird spoke to my father, saying, "I am the Thunder Maker, and my name is Many Drums. You have witnessed my great power and can now go in safety. When you return to your people, make a pipe just like the one you saw me smoking and add it to your bundle. Whenever you hear the first thunder rolling in the springtime, you will know that I have come from my cavern and that it is time to take out my pipe. If you should ever be caught in the midst of a heavy thunderstorm and feel afraid, pray to me, saying, "Many Drums! Pity me, for the sake of your youngest child, and no harm will come to you." (This prayer is often used by the Blackfeet during a dangerous storm.)

As soon as my father returned, he added to his medicine bundle a pipe similar to the one shown to him by the Thunder-bird.

—Curtis, *The North American Indian*, 6:67

themselves from lightning, the Long-time Pipe was transferred to new keepers, relatives of George and Molly Kicking Woman.

G. G. Kipp notes that all of the principal transfers of knowledge and healing powers came from what are now Glacier and Waterton Lakes National Parks or have strong associations with the area. Chief Mountain, Lakes Inside (St. Mary Lakes), and Waterton Lakes are the spiritual source areas for the bundles. So the park itself gave us some of the very, very richest ceremonies of our people. These ceremonies actually form our culture, our religion, and our thought.[12]

Medicine

Pauline Matt, a contemporary plant gatherer, explains that for the Blackfeet, medicine is everything around us, not the medicine that you go to the hospital or the clinic to get. "To us," she said, "medicine is life, something we get from all aspects of life, but something we can also give back. For example," she said, standing on a ridge along the Two Medicine River, "there's a red rock right here behind me. That is medicine. If one of your family members is sick, one of the best things to bring them is a little

Pauline Matt gathering traditional medicinal plants in 2009 Sally Thompson, photographer

The Vision Quest

▶ ▶ ▶ ▶ ▶ ▶ ▶ ◈ ◀ ◀ ◀ ◀ ◀ ◀ ◀

FINDING one's power is hard to do. First, the one to seek power must have a sweat bath to cleanse the body. You have to do this four consecutive days and nights, praying all the time. You must then leave the camp and go out where no one else is around. No matter where you go, there is a power spirit there. Spirits are up in the mountains, trees, rivers. All animals have supernatural spirits; the birds too.

When seeking a spirit, you must pray at all times. And you must take with you certain things that are necessary to the quest: a pipe, tobacco, a flint and striker, some dry moss, and, most importantly, incense.

The quest for a vision or seeking a power is no easy task. Even after you find the right location for the quest, you must be sure you are several days away from any other human being, you must be alone. In this way, the supernatural spirit shall test you for your bravery, and if you stand the test, then shall you receive that power.

You will have not food because you have to be humble and act pitiful. You will have no food for four days. If a spirit comes and gives you the power within the four days, then you will have food and water. Remember! No food or water, just your smoking, your burning of incense, and your prayers. If the vision is achieved within the four days, then you can eat, but only after you have taken four more sweat baths to purify your body.

—Adapted from Percy Bullchild's description in *The Sun Came Down*, 77–79

red rock because it helps them in healing. That rock has its own healing powers. When I go out to give offerings, I'll give my offerings to the sun and thank the sun for all the life it provides us with. When the early explorers came in, they thought we were praying to the sun and that's when they insisted that the Christians needed to . . . help civilize our people because they believed that we were just being crazy praying to all of the elements of the earth and water."[13]

Medicine comes to people in various forms. It can come in a dream and give a person the right to collect a certain plant or paint. Or a person can seek out medicine through fasting and prayer. To achieve medicine power this way, one must follow rules of the vision quest taught to the people long ago by the Creator.

Earth paints are basic and essential to all the ceremonies of the Blackfeet. Red is the most important paint, along with black, yellow, white, and the rare blue paint. Our most important red paint is found in Glacier Park.

We don't reveal the location. Only certain people have the right to collect the paints and know the protocols to do so.

Buffalo stones, *iniskim,* another important medicine, are fossils shaped like buffalo. One of these stones sang to a woman long, long ago to help her call in the buffalo during a time of great hunger. Iniskim have served the people ever since. When someone acquires an iniskim, a medicine person will bless it in a ceremony where the old song is sung and the buffalo stone, along with the owner's hands and face, is painted with prepared red paint. Traditional people still carry a buffalo stone.

Blackfeet iniskim, or buffalo stones Glacier National Park, HPF 4758

Medicinal plants are the oldest form of medicines, cures, and remedies used by our people. Creator showed Mudman, the first man, all about plant medicines by uprooting several kinds of plants. And as he pulled each one up, he named it and told Mudman what it was for, what sickness it would heal. He took Mudman into the woods. He showed him the bark of certain trees, the sap of some of the bushes, and certain berries that were for medical use. After he had shown him all the many different leaves, barks, roots, saps, berries, and certain weeds and told him what sicknesses they were good for, he taught Mudman how to apply them to the one who was being doctored.[14]

As Darnell Rides At The Door explains:

> Plants are both food and medicine found everywhere. This area, geographically speaking, is both abundant and proficient in providing us with what we need. . . . Our teachers . . . were our grandmothers and grandfathers that have gone before us. They taught us how to gather, prepare, and administer in the proper and respectful manner, emphasizing that we remember the power of each medicine and use it respectfully. We have two categories of medicines: holy medicines, those that are given to worthy

individuals through dreams or sacred transfer, and common medicines, those that are widely used. At one time, everyone knew how to use certain medicines from the land to keep the mind, body, and spirit healthy.[15]

Pauline Matt explains that the most important aspect of gathering plants is spiritual:

> We never go out and gather any of our plants without taking along our tobacco and our smudges. It's a way of honoring our Creator, our God, and showing the Creator that we're humble people, that we come to gather this plant with the deepest respect.
>
> I was taught that when you go to gather a particular plant, the first plant you see is called the Grandmother plant, and she'll show herself to you. . . . The minute you look at those plants she'll stand out, and so to her you give your offering . . . and you ask her for the right to take the life force of this plant. . . . The plants around her are called the relatives. To them too, I give offerings. . . .
>
> After I give my offerings to the Grandmother and to the relatives, if there are just very few plants around, I won't gather that plant. But still I've acknowledged them and honored them for being there. That . . . ensures that these plants are always going to be here; they won't be extinct. I won't be a greedy gatherer.
>
> The bear is the one that comes to us in our dreams to teach us about the plants. I think if I was more spiritually devoted like our ancestors, I would learn more.[16]

Sky Watchers and Record Keepers

In our Blackfeet world, before adapting to the European notion of twelve solar months divided into four seasons, we knew where we were in the great cosmos by carefully observing natural patterns. Without watches, we knew what time it was at night by watching the position of the Big Dipper, remembering the legend of how Moon, angry at her husband, the Sun, and their children, the Seven Boys, chases them around and around. They never stop. Their chase is the basis for the movement of time. "How is the last brother pointing?" meant "What time is it?" This question referred to the position of the Seven Brothers as they swing across the northern sky. The direction of the handle changes through the night, pointing down to the horizon just before dawn.

Before clocks and calendars, we recognized fourteen moons, divided equally between the two seasons, summer and winter. Beaver Men, the keepers of the Beaver Bundles, had the responsibility of keeping track of the moons and seasons. One of the methods to keep track was by notching sticks, one notch for each night on a stick that represented one moon. Fourteen carved sticks, painted half red and half black, represented the moons. G. G. Kipp explains that the Beaver Men turned a stick over at the passing of each moon. Once seven had been turned, winter was over and summer was beginning.[17] Another method to track time was with strings. At the beginning of the New Year, marked by the first snow, Beaver Men would cut fourteen fresh buckskin strings, keeping these with their sacred bundles. Each evening, they would tie a knot in the buckskin string for that moon. Sometimes a shell or a bead marked the four days of the new moon, what we called "moon opening" days.

Richard Sanderville and Yellow Kidney told Claude Schaeffer that another method for reading the number of winter months was to examine the liver of a porcupine. For each month of winter, a fatty lump called a "jabe" would grow on a porcupine's liver, until seven lumps marked the end of that season.[18] When a porcupine was killed, people asked, "How many more months of winter?" In this northerly latitude, winter is the time when nights are longer than days. The return of the longer days of summer, when daylight exceeds the dark, is welcomed by all.

Seven is a very important number in our cosmology, as is the number four. Seven days complete each quarter of the moon's cycle, and seven boys make up the stars of the Big Dipper. Each moon can be seen for twenty-six days, and then it's hidden from view for four days, with the midpoint at twenty-eight, four times seven. Creator Sun did the work of creation during the four-day periods, when the angry moon wouldn't see him. These four-day "moon openings" continue to be the times when many ceremonial activities are conducted.

Before the coming of the white men, those who kept traditional calendars also remembered special events, such as the deaths of relatives and chiefs, notable raids or battles with enemies, and famines and illnesses. Sometimes these events were added to the buckskin strings with separate double knots. Each full year was recorded in this way, the keeper designating it by the title of the year's major event rather than by numbers like we use today. Such yearly records are known as "winter counts."

The more familiar form of winter count is the documentation of the memorable events by recording an image on a tanned buffalo hide, one

The winter count symbol for 1779 noted the year when it hailed in the winter. Paul M. Raczka, *Winter Count: A History of the Blackfoot People* (Brocket, Alta.: Oldman River Cultural Centre, 1979), 25

symbol for the selected event to mark the year. Few Blackfeet winter counts have been documented. One North Piegan winter count published in a book by Paul Raczka was kept by five men who painted the images on hide. The drawings include the period from 1764 through 1924. Notable events during these years included such things as severe weather occurrences and unusual natural phenomena, such as the year when it hailed in winter.[19]

A winter of bad storms also occurred in the 1850s. Walter McClintock learned of this during the stormy winter of 1896–1897, when he heard "the booming of a bursting tree, and then of a water-filled hollow." His companion and interpreter, Siksikai-koan (Billy Jackson), told McClintock that those were signs of more bad weather, as he remembered hearing about such signs from an earlier time. He said, "My friend Bear Paw, who lives near the mountains, says it is over forty years since we had a moon with such bad storms. Before they came, he saw a mysterious ball of fire hang over the forest. Bear Paw keeps tribal records on buffalo skins: deaths of chiefs, cold winters, summers of drought and of plenty."[20]

We watch the night sky to know where we are in the unfolding seasons and to remember where we came from. The relationship between the moon and the stars is culturally embedded on our tipi flaps, with Seven Persons (the Big Dipper) on the north side and Lost Children (the Pleiades) on the south side.

Brings Down the Sun told of the cycling seasons and how the people learned by paying attention to all the life around them:

> My father taught me how to read the future, by watching the flights of birds and the habits of wild animals. Of all the birds, we look upon the raven as the wisest. When I see one soaring over our camp, I know a messenger is coming from a distance. If two ravens sit near a trail with their heads close together, it is a sign an

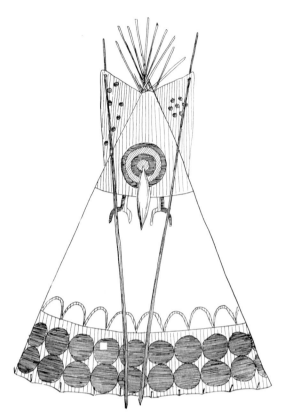

Three Bears created the Winter Painted Tipi after being caught in a blizzard. The design had come to him in a vision while weathering the storm. Clark Wissler, *Ceremonial Bundles of the Blackfoot Indians* (New York: American Museum of Natural History Trustees, 1912), 235

enemy is near. On a hunt, if I see a flock of ravens playing together, I go in that direction and am sure to find game.

My father taught me to read the signs in the sky—if the sun paints his face (sun dogs), a big storm is coming; when the "fires of the northmen" (the aurora) show in the sky, a heavy wind is coming; a "feeding star" (a comet) is a sign of famine and sickness; and if the sun hides his face (an eclipse), a great chief is about to die. The rainbow is the "lariat"; it is the Thunder roping the rain, and the storm will slow up.[21]

This knowledge is not forgotten. Many of us have learned from our grandparents about weather forecasting by observing cloud formations and how they sit in the west toward evening. As an old woman, Mary Ground, partially blind, told her granddaughter, Darnell Rides At The Door, "Look up there to the mountains and describe the clouds to me."

From her grandmother, Darnell learned that if you see clouds that look like "mare's tails," it's going to be windy. Big fluffy clouds will bring thunder and hail. Black clouds in winter come before the chinook.

Other weather information can be gleaned from observing nature. If it's raining and you see horses playing, the storm will continue. A double sun dog indicates an extreme change of weather. "Tipi liners" are those clouds that settle in the mountains. When they appear, the weather will change. Arlene Augare explains that the word for these clouds in Blackfeet

Blackfeet elder Mary Ground was more than one hundred years old when photographed in 1987.
Glacier National Park, HPF 2869

means "holding something back." "If the fall and winter are very foggy, creating that thick frost in winter," Cynthia Kipp warns, "watch for a real wet spring."[22]

Stormmaker's Tipi

▶ ▶ ▶ ▶ ▶ ▶ ▶ ◈ ◀ ◀ ◀ ◀ ◀ ◀ ◀

IN the beginning, when Creator made First Old Man, Omak Kinah, and First Old Woman, Mah Doo Wa Aki, he gave Napi the responsibility to look after them. Napi was Creator's helper and did many tasks and deeds in the beginning. Napi was first instructed to stay close to First Old Man and First Old Lady. At that time, they had no shelter, so when Storm Maker came with Cold and Wind and winter was coming, they shivered from the cold and huddled close to their cooking fire. Napi saw them and began to think of how he could get them shelter. A wisp of wind blew a large yellow leaf from the cottonwood tree on to the top of Napi's head. "*Ashw* (yes)," thought Napi, "this is a good way to build a shelter."

From then on, all our *Natooyis* were shaped like Napi's first tipi. Napi gathered the things that he needed to make a tipi: buffalo skins for the cover, ash wood for the pegs, chokecherry sticks for the buttons, lodgepole pine for the poles, rawhide rope to fasten the poles and hold up the liners, and a calfskin door. Napi taught First Old Man and First Old Lady how to pitch their tipi. They were told to pitch it so that the first rays of sun coming up would shine through the door for warmth.

As time went on, all descendants of the first ones became the Pikunni Nation. Every family lived in its own tipi. Napi told us to make a circle of all tipis and to have a doorway for the rising sun. That is why we camp that way to this day.

—This story has long been told us by our elders.

The new moon is another conveyor of weather information—the shape at the top of the sliver will tell if it's going to be dry or wet. Old-time Blackfeet would be able to tell if it's going to rain a lot or be colder from the shape of the moon.

Brings Down the Sun told Walter McClintock of his father's way of knowing the world:

> My father used to lie beside the fire on long winter evenings, giving me instructions, and recounting the interesting events that happened during his life. He taught me how to look into the future by observing the warnings of the animals, and how to know the different moons, which enabled him to keep his records, by watching the changes in the seasons, and by studying the habits of birds and wild animals.[23]

In the days when buffalo still roamed the land, we knew when to travel and when not to travel and knew where different foods would be ready, and our travels were dictated by this cycle. The buffalo was most important, but

Blackfeet elder Brings Down the Sun,
ca. 1900 Walter McClintock, photographer, Yale Collection of Western Americana, Beinecke Rare Book and Manuscript Library, Yale University, New Haven, Connecticut, 1089906

particular camp locations were selected with other resources in mind as well. To an observer, the changes in camp locations through the year may appear random, but they were far from that. Each location was known for the resources it held, whether they were plant, animal, or mineral, and year after year, our people returned to these locations.

The seasonal round presented here will take you back to our buffalo days. We are grateful to our elders for preserving stories about this long-ago way of living. Some of these stories have been passed down through our families, and some details about food-gathering techniques were shared with anthropologists and other visitors, who recorded them. We share them here with you.

Around the Seasons

Our sacred geography shows us our path through life. By following this path, our people will live long and productive lives.
—Nitsitapiisinni, *Story of the Blackfoot People*, 49

Just like north is arbitrary for the top of a map, January 1 and the winter solstice are both culturally determined times for the New Year, not universal facts. We Blackfeet begin our annual cycle when life wakes up again after the long winter. For us, this is the beginning of the New Year.

Saiaiksi Otsitaotohpi (March), or "When the Geese Return"

Also known as "Napi Comes Running Down Off of the Mountains," "Warm Chinook Winds," "Gopher," and "Time for Sore Eyes" (caused by snow blindness)

Imagine springtime arriving two hundred years ago, before treaties, reservations, and railroads changed this world so dramatically; before the buffalo were destroyed. The excitement of new life was everywhere, just as it is today, except more so. Imagine skies darkened by enormous flocks of returning birds. In early March each year, even today, tens of thousands of snow geese and whistler swans migrate through Blackfeet country on their way north. The Canada geese come and stay, the curlew appears, and snow turns to rain. The air smells different. Green will soon replace the white of winter.

(following pages) Snow geese Courtesy Bryony Schwan, photographer

In the Blackfeet world, the New Year begins when signs of life emerge after the long winter. The storytelling season ends, and preparations for the arrival of Thunder are underway. When the ice starts to break up—the time that the beavers leave their dens—the Beaver Bundle keepers begin their preparations for opening the bundle.

The change from winter to summer can come as early as March or as late as May depending upon the year, and when it does, the beauty of green life is seen again. In the old days, everyone anticipated the great variety of fresh foods after having eaten a diet dominated by meat and dried foods throughout the long winter. Our ancestors would eagerly gather great quantities of the new foods for spring feasts.

Bird eggs were a welcome spring treat. The season for collecting eggs lasted several months. With the early nesting season of geese, the people enjoyed those eggs first, taking care to collect only what was needed and not to disturb the viability of the clutch.

Young people got restless in this season before fresh buffalo became available again, and they ate all sorts of foods, as we know from our elders:

> When the buffalo was far, the girls would cut a big tree over there. . . . [A girl] would go up to it . . . [and] knock off the bark. . . . She would hit [the tree] lightly. Then she would peel [the bark] . . . [and] would tear [it] in two. She would eat it. It was very sweet. Then the girls and boys—many of them—would go . . . [o]ver there on the hill-side [and dig] for false roots [a kind of edible root], rattle-sound-roots, [and] make-bleed-roots. Those they ate also. The children never became sick. They would find the other [trees] to eat, they took all those trees. They peeled the bark from them. . . . They ate also roseberries and hard-seed-berries. And then there was earth-medicine [black alkali]. . . . They licked it. All the[ir] mouths would be . . . white from it. That [earth-medicine] prevented them from being sick.[24]

Matsiyi Kaapis Atoosi (April), or "Ice Breaking Up"

*Also known as "Frog Month," "Long Time Rain,"
and "Returning Bluebirds"*

When the ice started to break up, it was time for the Beaver Men to get ready to open the bundle. The loon is the first bird to come out of the Beaver Bundles, while the raven is the leader bird for the Thunder Bundles. These birds are the leaders of the Above Beings and Water Beings, respectively. They're very wise. Prairie chickens, eagles, chickadees, and other birds are honored in the beaver ceremony through imitative dances to express longevity and appreciation for continuity of the cycle of life.

When the Blackfeet still grew their native tobacco, there was a relationship between the timing of the tobacco planting and the beaver ceremony. As Mad Wolf explained to Walter McClintock, "We always give a beaver ceremony in the spring, when the tobacco seeds are planted; also because spring is the time when beavers are accustomed to leave their winter dens. . . . We first hold the beaver ceremony, and then dig up the ground with sharp-pointed sticks."[25]

Mad Wolf explaining Pikunni ways to Walter McClintock, 1905 Glacier National Park, GLAC4368

Traditional tobacco is no longer planted in this ceremonial fashion. The last tobacco planting ceremony was in 1966 among the Siksika in Alberta. Even so, tobacco remains an important part of the ritual life of the Blackfeet people, with smoke serving as an intermediary, carrying prayers to the Creator.

Plant foods were a welcome gift each spring, after a winter of meat and dried stores. The spring beauty, or wild potato, was known as lumpy-head (*Pach-op-it-skinni*) to the Blackfeet. This root was first available on the prairie and soon thereafter in the foothills. Women would dig lumpy-heads with a wooden stick or elk antler and then boil them for all to enjoy. Darnell Rides At The Door bemoans the small size of these little

*Spring beauty, also called
lumpy-head by the Blackfeet*
Jacqueline Moore, artist

potatoes now, "as small as the tip of your little finger," she says. "They're smaller because they are no longer in relationship with people; they're not being harvested."[26]

What the Blackfeet call *Po-kint-somo,* or wild rhubarb, is commonly known as cow parsnip. In spring, roasted stalks of this plant added variety and flavor to the diet. Many of the Pikunni people still look forward to these tasty seasonal treats. Children also will make a whistle with the stalks or wait until fall and eat the soft white insides.

Depending on the season, other greens and roots may ripen in April as well. Greens include elk thistle and dandelion. Some important roots include balsamroot, glacier lily, yellowbell, and prairie parsley. A treat for children this time of year was to pick and suck the sweet stems of shooting stars, known as "Indian Candy."

Duck eggs were especially important spring food. Claude Schaeffer's field notes include details about egg gathering and cooking from elders who remembered these activities:

> [A] quantity of duck eggs were broken and contents dropped into the heart sac of a bison. The container was tied at the mouth and then dropped into a kettle of boiling water to cook the egg yolks. Eggs for eating could be transported more easily in this way than fragile eggs. . . . The eggs of the crow, coot, magpie, hawk, ducks, cranes, etc., were eaten. Swans nested farther north.[27]

Glacier lily Jacqueline Moore, artist

Other spring activities included gathering chokecherry wood to make bows and arrows, and trapping golden eagles as they returned from the south. Remains of an old eagle-trapping pit were found by Old Sun on a butte in the general vicinity of Lower Two Medicine Lake.[28] Claude Schaeffer made note of what the elders told him about eagle trapping:

> [A] pit . . . beneath a butte about four feet long was dug. Earth carried some distance away and scattered about. Sod replaced about pit.
>
> As bait a wolf skin was stuffed and covered with fresh blood and fat. It was then placed on top of pit. Bait would first be discovered by magpies and crows, which flocked about. Eagle, seeing these, would be attracted. The trapper would hear it alright. It would start to feed upon neck meat, which was too tough for smaller birds. Eagle pulled through by both legs, its back broken and shoved on shelf scratched out on side of pit.
>
> Trapper said to hoot like an owl, if inferior or young birds caught. Caws, like crow, if birds with good feather secured.
>
> A lodge is made of cottonwood boughs, where a ceremony is held. Young girls and boys dance, in order that birds of that

year will be caught. Each time that dead eagles are brought there, pemmican is stuffed in their beaks. Birds allowed to be there until partly decomposed, then feathers easier to remove.

Thirty-six feather (three tails) equal the value of one horse in trade.

The long trailing war bonnet called by the term meaning "boss-ribs.[29]

Eagle feathers represent long life, energy, power, accomplishment, or coups. Buffalo boss ribs are the "staff of life" for the Blackfeet people. Both eagle feathers and buffalo boss ribs are signified in the flag of the Blackfeet Nation.

Eagles are extremely important to Indian people—and to Blackfeet, in particular, because, according to our ancestors, eagles get a second chance at life. After three decades of living, their talons get too hard and long and their beaks get worn down, and they come to a time when they can't hunt. At that time, they have a choice to make. If they choose to live, they go back to where they were born. Here, they smash off their talons and smash off their beaks, and then they have to survive the month it takes for replacements to grow in. If they make it, they've won a second chance at living another thirty years. This is one reason why eagle feathers are so important to us. We also honor them because they have touched the clouds where a human being has not reached.

Each time our men bravely risked their lives, they were awarded another feather for their war bonnet. In the old days, it took a long time to earn the feathers of a war bonnet.

Otsikists (May), or "The Buffalo Flower Grows"

Also known as "Leaves Coming Out,"
"Last Snow Storm," and "Green Grass"

Just when the people start to enjoy the warmer and longer days of spring, when the mists rise off of the flowing streams and the sounds of geese, swans, and ducks fill the air, the big storm hits. The Blackfeet word for this big storm is *mawh-cape-bee*. At this time, "when horses begin to shed their winter hair," a storm would come "out of the blue," bringing winds from all directions and blowing snow into deep drifts over the prairie. Sometimes these deep, wet snows obscured the terrain so that buffalo fell off snow-covered cutbanks and died, providing easy meals.

Buffalo cow nursing her calf R. Butterfield, photographer, Glacier National Park, 9479

Not until after this predictable spring storm was spent was it time for people to prepare to leave the winter camps. In buffalo days, the time to leave the long camps of winter was signaled by the flowering of the "buffalo plant," or false lupine. The blooming of these yellow flowers reminded the people that the buffalo cows had dropped their calves, whose new coats were yellow.

Thunder Pipe ceremonies were conducted to honor the return of Thunder, whose home is Chief Mountain. That's where the first Thunder Pipe was given to the people. The family responsible for the Blue Thunder Lodge would raise it when they heard the first thunder. This lodge came from "the Backbone of the World," the high mountains of the main chain of the Rockies, and is known as a "fair weather lodge." The ritual was given as a protection from storms and has power to clear the sky. The eastern edges of what is now Glacier Park have always provided the Blackfeet with their lodge poles. Whereas Thunder usually returns around April, it might arrive as early as March or as late as June. In the year of the Glacier National Park centennial, 2010, the Thunder Pipe Bundle ceremonies were held in June because of the late arrival of Thunder.

As new grass emerged and frogs were heard croaking in the spring ponds, the buffalo would move out onto the prairie, away from the more broken landscape near the mountains. Then the Blackfeet would also move

Blackfeet women scraping a hide for tanning, 1904 Walter McClintock, photographer, Yale Collection of Western Americana, Beinecke Rare Book and Manuscript Library, Yale University, New Haven, Connecticut, 1098249

away. In preparation for moving camp, men cut new lodge poles, often on Cutbank Creek, on Lower St. Mary Lake, and below Running Eagle Falls, and women completed new lodge covers.

When the camp leaders, the bundle keepers, gave the word that it was time to move, women would pack up their lodges, carefully condensing these massive covers to fit onto the travois, along with small children and all the rest of the household gear. Tipis in those days

> were made from the heavy hides of the moose, elk, and buffalo. The hair was scraped off and processed with the brain of the animal, then soaked in water until soaked through. Then it was worked back and forth across a rough edge of a rock, or something with a sharp edge. This was a continual work to the finish, because the hide had to be dry and soft while you're working on it. If one quits work on it [too soon] . . . , the hide will dry hard and stiff. It is important to stay with the work until the hide is soft and dry.[30]

It took approximately fifteen or sixteen buffalo hides to make an eighteen-foot-diameter tipi. This size tipi required at least twenty-one poles. Four main poles created the basis for the structure, with two poles used to adjust the ear flaps. It is said that the four main poles that created the quadrapod represented the four major bands of the Blackfeet. The rest of the poles form a conical cohesive structure that binds all the people in unity. To make a tipi out of hides, one had to be skilled in the tanning process: to know when to harvest the hide and how to mathematically compute the pattern to form a conical structure that was both warm in the winter and cool in the summer and had air drafts, flumes, and liners. The tipi also had to be waterproof and windproof. And be livable.

A tipi was constructed, furnished, and taken care of by the women; therefore, the female owned the home. This procedure took a season to complete. Smoking the hides made them waterproof to keep out the elements of water and snow. A certain procedure with the tie-down rope would create a water outlet, as well as the outside structural setting, based on the use of a ditch around the perimeter and certain tree branches.

At early ages, young females learned the skill of tanning and smoking the hides, the method of constructing the tipis, and the art of pitching them. Generations of skilled women, young and old, formed this

Blackfeet women sewing the hides for a lodge Walter McClintock, photographer, Yale Collection of Western Americana, Beinecke Rare Book and Manuscript Library, Yale University, New Haven, Connecticut, 1098910

workforce. Every new day was a learning experience. Skill, strength, good health, and physical fitness were natural outcomes of the long hours of hard work. The tools and implements came from the buffalo and other animals. Everything used in the lodge was from nature, right down to the sinew used to sew the hides together. McClintock's sources told him:

> It was an Indian custom to go every spring to the forests on the mountains, to cut new lodge-poles for their summer camps. . . . We cut the straight and slender trees of lodge-pole pine for tepee poles, peeling off the bark and standing them in the sun to dry. The women also gathered plants and herbs in meadow and forest, both for eating and healing.[31]

During a warm May, the Blackfeet gathered nature's bounty. When the sweet perfume of wolf willow flowers was in the air, early fruits added to the variety of spring foods. For vegetables, the people gathered wild onions, wild potatoes, cow parsnip, bitterroot, and prairie turnip. But the camas was their favorite vegetable. It had a root like a small potato and a sweet flavor. They roasted the stalks of the cow parsnip when they were tender and juicy in the spring. Bundle holders enjoyed these plant foods along with everyone else, but they were restricted in the animal foods they could consume, being limited to those species not represented in their bundle.

This time of year, the Blackfeet dried the leaves of bearberry and *pipsissewa* (also known as princess pine) for tobacco. They used a lichen that grows on pine trees as yellow dye, a pore fungus for cleaning buckskin, and yellow *Orthocarpus* for dyeing skins. For eye inflammation, they used the blossoms of horsemint, the long-plumed avens for coughs, Oregon grape for stomach trouble, and gum plant for the liver.[32]

The round, edible mushrooms known as puffballs signify the "dusty stars" on the bottom of Blackfeet tipis and were considered to be important beings. In one important legend, the puffball, whose parents are Morning Star and Feather Woman, was transformed into the North Star. Puffballs were used for many purposes. As a punk, they worked better than bark kindling.

> Indian boys wore a bandolier of puffballs across their chests to ward off respiratory diseases. The soft central portion of dried immature puffballs was bound on wounds to stop bleeding and was held on the eye to remove foreign objects. The powdery interior of ripe puffballs was used on wounds and was applied to

Blackfeet Buffalo Lodge with puffball-shaped "dusty stars" around the bottom, 1905
Walter McClintock, photographer, Yale Collection of Western Americana, Beinecke Rare Book and
Manuscript Library, Yale University, New Haven, Connecticut, 1089828

the umbilicus of newborn babies. Spores were snuffed to stop
nosebleed. Puffballs were used to decorate the tipi cover. A dark-
colored band at the base of certain tipis represented earth; circular
objects in or arising out of the dark-colored band were puffballs
and represented life in or arising out of the earth.[33]

New sweat lodges were erected once the camp was settled. Building
sweat lodges of willow branches was the work of men, following a very
specific protocol. People sweated year-round (and many of our people still
do). Cleansing has always been an important preparation for ceremony.
Only men participated in this cleansing ritual. Women supported them by
closing down or opening the doors and offering prayers and support outside the lodge. Their duties varied depending on the time of year. People
also sweated before leaving with a war party or a horse-capturing party
and again when they returned. Anyone questing for a vision would first
go through the four rounds in the sweat lodge. This practice continues to
be important.

Blackfeet sweat lodge Walter McClintock, photographer, Yale Collection of Western Americana, Beinecke Rare Book and Manuscript Library, Yale University, New Haven, Connecticut, 1098017

In Blackfeet country, first fruits are the bearberry and the gooseberry. Cambium could be harvested from cottonwoods at this time, when the sap was running. Black tree lichen was gathered as well for use as a dye and to treat headaches.

Two types of bitterroot were gathered—the common type, the larger of the two, known as "bitter root," and a smaller variety known as "white root." Blackfeet traded for the former root with the west-side tribes and sometimes went to war for this important, highly nutritious and sustaining food. The latter was ritually added to savisberry soup for Thunder Pipe ceremonies.[34]

In the spring, as snow melted and higher elevation areas opened up, the men hunted in the lower mountains for deer while the women gathered their plant foods and medicines. The headwaters of the South Fork of the Milk River provided good hunting opportunities. The people favored elk and deer, but they would hunt sheep, goats, and moose as well. According to Percy Bullchild,

The early people carried lunch, too, whenever necessary. . . . The lunch might consist of dried meat and dried back fat, *oo-suc*. Most generally, the liver of a large animal, such as an elk, a moose, or a buffalo, was cooked right in the hot coals of an open fire. While cooking, the top part of the liver hardens into a crust and burns almost total black, but the inside of it is cooked nice, juicy, and soft. This liver keeps for several days without spoiling. . . . A few bites of the roasted liver will last for many hours without one getting hungry.[35]

When the time was right and the grasses were green, extended family groups would split apart to follow the buffalo and other game out onto the grassy plains, always choosing campsites near good water and firewood. Although four-legged animals predominated, birds also contributed to the diet. Grouse were secured during the season of their mating dance. A special dance imitates the prairie chickens in the beaver ceremony.

Misomsootayi (June), or "The Long Rains Come"

*Also known as "Time of High Waters," "Moon of Hatching,"
and "Savisberry Begins to Ripen"*

June was (and is) a beautiful time of year and affirmed the return of abundance, with a wide variety of plant foods and medicines ripe and ready for consumption. Roots were a particularly important part of the diet, bringing essential vitamins and minerals up from the ground to keep people healthy. Most roots were dried for storage and future use.

Digging the tasty camas roots was work that the women enjoyed. Although not as important to the Blackfeet as to the Kootenais, these nutritious additions to the diet were always welcomed. A good source of camas was located along Cutbank Creek. The roots of American bistort, edible either raw or fire roasted, were gathered in the foothills and mountains and used in soups and stews. We call them *ek-sik-a-pato-api*, or "looks back." This plant should not be confused with water smartweed, which is poisonous and looks like bistort but will sting your tongue if you eat this one by mistake!

In addition to camas and bistort, the women gathered a variety of roots and herbs, such as wild onions, called *pesat-se-nekim*, or "funny vine," which were eaten raw and were also used for flavoring; mint leaves, which were dried and stored to flavor and preserve meat and were also used for a tea; bitterroot, which continued to be available at higher elevations; wild turnip, which was common in the area and an important food; and Canadian milk vetch, known as tender root, which was found on gravel bottoms or prairie slopes throughout the eastern part of the Blackfeet territory. This root was gathered in spring or fall and eaten raw or boiled in water and also dried for winter use. It has a flavor more appealing to children than many of the root foods, which tend to be somewhat bitter.[36]

The tobacco seeds sprouted while the people were off hunting buffalo. Some of the important men who were responsible for the well-being of the tobacco would return to the garden to tend the plants several times during the growing season. According to Mad Wolf, "If the season is dry and the tobacco needs rain, I take the otter-skin from the Beaver Bundle and tie it to a pole. It floats in the wind and is sure to bring rain."[37]

Late spring was a time to feast on waterfowl eggs. Children would sometimes swim out into lakes to collect the eggs. George Bird Grinnell noted that after a large quantity of eggs had been gathered,

> a hole was dug in the ground, and a little water put in it. At short intervals about the water, platforms of sticks were built, on which the eggs were laid. A smaller hole was dug at one side of the large hole, slanting into the bottom of it. When all was ready, the top of the larger hole was covered with mud, laid upon cross sticks, and red-hot stones were dropped into the slant, when they rolled down into the water, heating it, and so cooking the eggs by steam.[38]

According to Yellow Kidney, the eggs of the coot (*aks ksissi*), plentiful at this time of year, were considered especially good. They were collected from nests in the reeds by children and piled on shore.

> One of the boys then removed a legging. One end of it was tied shut and the bottom stuffed with dried grass. Then the eggs were placed inside in layers separated by others of dried grass to prevent breakage. Slough grass was then woven about the top of the emergency receptacle, the end tied and the whole bundle slung over the arm to be carried back to camp.[39]

If a large number of coot eggs had been collected, they were cooked in a rock-heated pit. The eggs were placed inside, in layers separated by dried grass. The pit was then filled with water, and heated rocks were placed near the edge to set the water boiling. They were lifted by the shoulder blade of a buffalo. Then the cooked eggs were removed. Dried buffalo tripe was filled with grass and used as a container to carry the eggs to camp.

Itohtoyiitotsiwamaata (July), or "When the People Move Together"

Also known as "Flower Moon," "Thunder Moon," and "Ripe Berries"

When the berries were ripe and the grass long, it was time to move to the circle camp for the Okan, the Medicine Lodge. The work of moving camp was the responsibility of the women, the owners of the lodges. When the head chief decided to move camp, that evening the camp crier would announce that in the morning everyone should be ready to leave. The women were up at dawn preparing the family breakfast, finishing packing, and tying the family belongings to the horse travois. Everyone was looking forward to "going home days," the ancient term used to refer to the move toward the place of the Okan.

A woman would take down her lodge and tie the poles between the horses' horned saddles. Two horses were needed to transport the lodge poles. Usually, the people stashed lodge poles at camps throughout their

When the summer camp was reached, Blackfeet women raised the lodge cover to wrap around the lodge poles. This image was taken in 1908. Walter McClintock, photographer, Yale Collection of Western Americana, Beinecke Rare Book and Manuscript Library, Yale University, New Haven, Connecticut, 1099035

Parade around camp before construction of the Okan lodge, 1908 Walter McClintock, photographer, Yale Collection of Western Americana, Beinecke Rare Book and Manuscript Library, Yale University, New Haven, Connecticut, 1090272(1)

territory, so they wouldn't have to drag so many poles over a long distance. They would arrive at their summer camp and find tipi poles where they had left them the previous year.

Women packed saddlebags filled with dried meat and berries, tallow, and tobacco, and they packed bedding, tools, utensils, and ceremonial objects to be carried on the travois. Babies rode on their mothers' backs while the toddlers rode on the travois. Older boys took care of the loose horses. Each day's journey would end early enough that the women could unpack and erect their lodges, cook supper, and then prepare for the next day before the stars appeared. Children helped gather wood, bring water, and tend the horses. When wood was low, women used dried buffalo chips for fire. One important task was to keep the fire going from one camp to the next. A hard fungus that grows on trees, called *apopikatiss,* meaning "makes-your-hair-gray," provided a container for carrying coals.

In preparation for the Okan, the people would acquire a hundred ceremonial buffalo tongues. These tongues were gathered over several weeks, rather than killing so many animals at one time. A special process was used, and still is, to prepare and preserve the tongues for the ceremony.

The Okan was a time of many activities and ceremonies. Deeds were recognized, new names were given, and families renewed kinship and friendship. "Going home days" was a joyous time of the year. Families were reunited, relatives old and new visited, and the company of others enjoyed. New babies were introduced to relatives, teens were given new names earned by the rite of passage to adolescence, and societies inducted new members. Sacred bundles were honored and opened. The Holy Woman's vow to sponsor the Okan was fulfilled, and all who could participate did so in the sacred lodge to the sun. With the center pole upright, the lodge constructed, and the dances successful, everyone was pleased that the people would have a good year.

After the Okan, the chief would tell his people it was time to move to "Many-berries," or other places rich in fruit. The women would gather *ok-kun-okin*, or savisberries, from tall shrubs that grow on hillsides and river bottoms. Savisberries, also known as serviceberries, sarvisberries, Juneberries, and saskatoons, are plentiful around Waterton Lakes and Glacier National Parks. These important berries have always been gathered in great quantities and added to stews, soups, and meat. In the old days, a large portion of the berries was dried and stored for future use. People took care not to eat too many fresh berries at a time or they would risk severe stomach pains.

Gathering berries, 1905 Walter McClintock, photographer, Yale Collection of Western Americana, Beinecke Rare Book and Manuscript Library, Yale University, New Haven, Connecticut, 1098404

Savisberries were mixed with ground-up dried meat and melted fat to make pemmican. "The mixture was shaped into small cakes and stored in rawhide containers to use during the winter and on journeys. Berry soup was made with either fresh or dried berries, the latter first soaked in water to make them soft. The berries were boiled in water, then turned into soup with the addition of pieces of meat, fat, wild turnip, or bitterroots."[40]

Serviceberry, also known as sarvisberry
Jacqueline Moore, artist

Gooseberries and red willow berries were also collected in late summer. The people would move from place to place because it was either a good location for picking berries or a good place to hunt bulbs. A variety of other plant foods and medicines were gathered during the summer. Wild turnip and tender roots continued to be gathered. Wild chives and other shoots remained accessible through the summer as well.

Additional plants of importance and their uses are detailed in *The Blackfoot Papers*:

> Wild parsley, or big turnip, "is a root that grows deep in the ground, with a plant growing one to two feet above, with yellow flowers. The roots were hard to dig up with only pointed wooden sticks. These were made of oiled, fire-hardened, highly polished, dried

berry wood or birch. One end of the digging stick was rounded and held against a thick piece of rawhide to protect the digger's stomach as she pushed the stick into the ground with the weight of her body. After they were gathered and peeled, these wild turnips were eaten raw or roasted, or else sun-dried for storage.

Yampa, called double root, "grows from one to three feet tall and has small, white flowers. Like other roots, it can be eaten fresh, after boiling, or dried for winter storage. A common way to prepare it for eating was to boil it in animal blood and then add sweetening." This important root, *neets ik-oop-ah,* tastes sweet and nut-like, a prized herb for diuretic purposes, sore throats, coughs. It was chewed for endurance and also used as a horse medicine. The Blackfeet call it "wild carrot" or "gopher turds."[41]

Medicines were widely available in summer. Bitter quinine, obtained from the red osier dogwood, for example, was mixed with savisberry to treat sore muscles and cramps. For every ailment, there existed at least one cure within this perfect homeland.

Summer was also a time for gathering other important resources. Sweetgrass was collected for incense. This plant is considered sacred and is highly prized by the Blackfeet. To capture the pure spirit of the sweetgrass

Yampa Jacqueline Moore, artist

takes concentration, prayer, and respect. If not done properly, the plant will hide from the gatherer. Much of the same goes for the sweet pine and other incense used by the people. One of these is juniper, a plant that takes at least two years to mature. Sage is also important: we do not burn it like other tribes do; for us, it is a cleanser as well as a medicine. You must gather it at a certain time before it goes to seed, and you must know the female and male plants.

Minerals were also gathered during the summer—after snows melted and rivers receded and they could be accessed. Men would go to source locations for flake-able stone to make their arrowheads and knives. Cobbles needed for smashing bone and other pounding and grinding chores could be collected from riverbeds once the water had receded. People knew exactly what stones to collect for each particular purpose. Black pipestone was another important item. A few sources of this pipestone occur within the Blackfeet territory, including an important source near East Glacier. Men would also trade for other stones or even for carved pipe bowls.

For the most part, women gathered the ochre to be mixed with oil for paint. The best time to gather paint was later summer when the spring runoff was past. Several paint sources are known in and around Glacier Park. Certain women knew the protocol for finding and gathering paint so as not to destroy its powers.

Salt is an important mineral to the mountain goat and other animals. The Blackfeet recognized this need and knew of locations for this mineral in the Glacier area.

Summer was an important time for vision seekers to go to the mountains for prayer and fasting. Over one hundred fasting beds, or vision quest sites, have been recorded by archaeologists in the two national parks, Glacier and Waterton Lakes.[42]

The curlew will usually leave about this time of year, migrating south, and giving an early sign that summer might not last much longer.

Pakkipistsi Otssitaitssp (August), or "When the Chokecherries Ripen"

*Also known as "Berry Moon," "End of the Medicine Lodge,"
and "Crows Begin to Bunch Up"*

As summer progressed, both waterfowl and various upland birds were taken for food. Waterfowl, according to Weasel Tail and recorded by

Claude Schaeffer, were taken in summer during nesting and molting seasons. Old women and children helped to chase molting birds and young waterfowl. According to Harry Under Mouse, the fledglings of wildfowl were closely watched by bird gatherers until the time they were almost ready to fly. Then groups of people would go to the lakes and, by throwing rocks, force the young birds to shore, where they were caught. This took place in August. One strategy, used at deep lakes to drive young birds to shore, was to burn buffalo chips along one shore. The smoke would drive the young birds to the opposite shore, where people were waiting. This drive procedure was known as *i-ta-wa-ki*.

Richard Sanderville provided more details about this fire drive:

> [P]eople used to take young ducks and geese, before they learned to fly. First [the men] pulled a hair from a robe and dropped in air, to determine direction wind was blowing. Men buil[t] a fire of buffalo chips. Pieces of burning chips were placed on surface of larger, deeper lakes, where waterfowl nested, so that wind would blow them towards opposite shore. . . . There, hidden hunters clubbed them. . . . [The d]uck feathers were used in stuffing pillows made from buckskin bags, and the wing and tail feathers were used by youths for fletching their arrow shafts.[43]

Many bird species were eaten at this time of year, including ducks, grouse (except ptarmigan), geese, cranes, swans, grebes, and blackbirds. Grebes were very fat and considered good eating. Some of these birds were not to be eaten by those responsible for the Thunder Bundles because they were represented in the bundles. Elders shared some of their memories about birds with Claude Schaeffer: "Young ducks, geese and other waterfowl," they said, "were cut in half, flattened and smoked over a fire."[44] A duck with a white breast was identified as the fattest variety. Fat from it was rendered out and stored in remnant bladders and used as an ointment. Children caught blackbirds, using a horsehair snare with crumbs as bait. Grouse (*kitoki*) were caught at the dancing place by placing a circle of willow hoops at runways and suspending a snare from it. Fool hens (*kitsitssim*) were taken with a pole snare or knocked from trees with clubs.

Yellow Kidney said that feathers of various hawks were used to feather arrow shafts. They split well for this purpose. Feathers kept for use as arrows were kept in a cylindrical container made of the untanned skin from the throat of a buffalo. The feathers were pushed through lacings to hold them tight in the receptacle.[45]

Blackfeet girls at play with a toy lodge, 1909 Walter McClintock, photographer, Yale Collection of Western Americana, Beinecke Rare Book and Manuscript Library, Yale University, New Haven, Connecticut, 03723008

Long ago, parties of men and women would travel into the foothills for smaller game. During this time, men would also hunt elk, deer, sheep, goats, and moose. They preferred elk and deer, but especially after the buffalo were gone, they would eat whatever they could obtain. The surplus meat was sliced, smoked, and stored away in parfleches for future use. Roots and berries were collected at the same time. Bearberries, rose hips, and white berries from the red willow were stored in "baby buffalo bags," or deer bags made from embryos. Foods of all these kinds were utilized during periods when buffalo could not be found.

August days were taken up with picking berries, especially huckleberries, and enjoying the bounty of the mountains. Cutbank Creek is a good place for huckleberries. People who hike in Glacier know that huckleberries are widespread and that they ripen later the higher you go. What a fine treat when you've hunted or hiked all day in the high country!

Other berries gathered in late summer included the berries of the red osier dogwood, fairy bells, wolf willow, and juniper. Along with wild plums, this variety of fruits provided a plentiful array of different flavors and nutrients. Although the chokecherries ripen at this time, the people waited until the first frost brought out their flavor before they picked them.

But all was not work. Summer games were many. Boys might be seen playing hoop-and-stick games, arrow games, or even a double-ball game, dreaming of becoming great hunters or warriors by imitating the men in sham battles. Girls might play a rock guessing game with rocks painted red and black or mimic adult women by making miniature dolls, tipis, and furnishings like "Mom's." Darnell Rides At The Door's grandmother remembered getting gopher hides and pressing into them with Indian paintbrush flowers to create a design on these small robes for the children. A heavy rock held the flower in place over a wet hide until the color set. Both girls and boys might play the run-and-scream game or the buffalo-jawbone gambling game.

Boy's summer game Nicholas Point, *Wilderness Kingdom, Indian Life in the Rocky Mountains: 1840–1847: The Journals and Paintings of Nicolas Point,* trans. Joseph P. Donnelly (New York, 1967), 65

Itowapipitssko (September), or "When the Leaves Turn Color"

*Also known as "Chokecherry Moon," "Long Time Rain,"
"Leaves Blown from Trees," "End of Summer Moon," "Departing of
Thunder," and "Moon That Dries Up Berries"*

At the time when "leaves are yellow and the time of first frost," the camp leader would announce that it was time to move to where the chokecherries were ready. The women would pick the fruit, then pound it with a stone maul, pits and all, and then dry it in small cakes. The Blackfoot name, *pukkiip,* or "crushed berry," comes from its mode of preparation. The hard seeds were crushed and ground into small grains.

Bullberries, or buffaloberries, were another important fruit of the fall. They were commonly added to soup. These bright red berries, like the

Napi Learns to Gather Bullberries

▶ ▶ ▶ ▶ ▶ ▶ ▶   ◈   ◀ ◀ ◀ ◀ ◀ ◀ ◀

ONE day Napi had nothing to do. He decided to go for a walk toward the river. When he got to the river, he saw some nice ripe bullberries. Napi wanted some of those berries, so he decided to dive into the water. He dove several times with no success. He couldn't reach the bottom of the river nor the berries.

Soon Napi decided to tie some rocks around his waist and feet. The rocks were heavy and helped him stay under the water. He stayed under for so long, he just about drowned. He tore the weights off and came up with no berries. Napi climbed out of the water and lay on the bank. As he was catching his breath, he looked up toward the sky and saw the bush of berries. They were not in the water after all. He realized that he had been diving at their reflection.

Napi was angry at the berries because they had caused him to almost drown. He got a big stick and began hitting the bush hard, and the berries began to fall. Soon there was a great pile of bullberries on the ground. And Napi told the bullberry bush, "From now on, this is the way

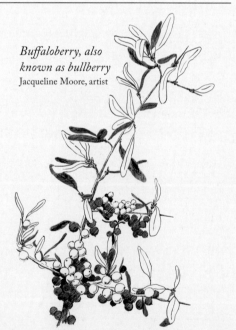

*Buffaloberry, also
known as bullberry*
Jacqueline Moore, artist

people will get bullberries. Because you are full of thorns, they will hit you with a stick instead of picking your berries by hand."

And this method is used even today.

—Rides At The Door, *Napi Stories,* 11

The Chokecherry

▶ ▶ ▶ ▶ ▶ ▶ ▶   ◈   ◀ ◀ ◀ ◀ ◀ ◀ ◀

CHOKECHERRIES grow on trees and ripen in early fall. They are not good to eat before they are fully ripe, and even then they are fairly tart. The proper preparation of chokecherries was quite an art. When fresh, they were boiled with water or fat, then sweetened to make soup. For storing, the cherries were crushed with stones and then dried in the sun. Grease had to be mixed with the ground cherries to keep them from drying too hard. The crushed cherries were formed into small cakes, like cookies, and placed on small sticks or turned regularly to keep them from spoiling on one side while they dried.

They were usually stored in bags made from small animal skins whose open legs were stuffed with mint, which kept the cherries from falling out and also allowed a little air to enter, preventing the contents from becoming moldy.

Pemmican was made by breaking up dried cherry cakes and soaking them in a bowl of water. When the cherries were soft, the water was strained out. This water, known as chokecherry brew, was a popular drink, especially in wintertime. The soaked cherries were then mixed with fat. Back fat was especially popular for this because it did not cake up easily. The fat-and-berry mixture was then pounded some more and was finally kneaded into small balls and served. These balls could also be placed in rawhide containers to be taken on hunting and war trips.

Blackfeet bow and arrows were made of chokecherry wood. Medicine pipestems, tripods for sacred bundles, and root-digging sticks were all made from chokecherry wood, which is so hard and tough that it will not soak up water, making an excellent fire starter after a hard rain.

Chokecherry stems were used in a variety of ways. Thin ones were stuck into roasting meat to add flavor, and bark scrapings were steeped to make a tea.

—Based on Hungry Wolf,
Blackfoot Papers, 1:130

Chokecherry Jacqueline Moore, artist

Tears-In-Her-Eyes in Blackfeet cradle Walter McClintock, photographer, Yale Collection of Western Americana, Beinecke Rare Book and Manuscript Library, Yale University, New Haven, Connecticut, 1090497

chokecherry, were gathered after the first frost. The shrubs grow along watercourses. The women and children collected these berries by beating the branches over a buffalo robe, careful not to get scraped by the long thorns.

Rose hips, like chokecherries and bullberries, were gathered after the first frost. The red fruits on wild rose bushes were thought of as "wild tomatoes." They could be eaten fresh from the bush and were commonly used that way as an emergency food since they remain on the bushes through most of the winter. Eating the seeds, however, causes an itchy rectum.

A meal of rose hips was made by boiling the fresh berries, crushing them up with fat, and then cooking the mixture on a "Black Plate," the Blackfeet name for a frying pan. The fried meal was then sweetened to taste. The berries were also boiled with a mixture of flour and sweetening to make a soup. Occasionally, for lack of other berries, rose hips were used in making pemmican. Rose hips had many uses, even as "Indian pacifiers" when placed inside a cloth for a baby to suck. Dried berries were also made into necklaces and used for trade items.[46] Cattail and sphagnum moss were gathered for diapering babies and for menstrual needs, held in place with a T-belt. Bistort, gathered in the fall, could also be used for these purposes. "Big white-root," a wild parsley, grows on the prairies. Ready to harvest in the early fall, it was eaten raw. The flavor is enhanced once it's dried.

In late summer and early fall, as the grasses dried up, the buffalo would move about in search of food. Blackfeet runners were always on the lookout for the buffalo, tracking their movements.

Buffalo herd in the fall Glacier National Park, 5323

When the summer season came to an end and the elders determined the right time, the camp crier would announce that the people should prepare to move to the wintering grounds in the valleys at the edge of the mountains. Everyone helped to prepare for travel. That night, they would feed their dogs and their horses well since these animals would work hard over the next several days while they traveled westward. Every one—children, women, and men—had a job to do while the people were on the move. Still, the men had time to hunt, the women to visit as they moved along, and the children to run and play on either side of the procession. This was their life; it was fun at times and heartbreaking at times.[47]

At this time, when the people returned to the mountain fringe, one anticipated activity was the ceremonial harvesting of tobacco. As Mad Wolf explained, "When the crop is ready, I call the people together. We put up a large tepee for a dance and have a feast which lasts four days and four nights. Then the Beaver Men pull up the plants. We mix the leaves with those of the bearberry (kinnikinnick), and distribute it among the people."[48]

Early fall was also the time of year when Beaver Bundles were asked for help to get through the winter. The bundles were opened. Prayers were offered, and tobacco pouches of the people who belong to the bundle were enclosed in the bundle for the winter. These offerings of tobacco were returned to the givers in the spring. Some Thunder Pipe Bundles were also opened, tobacco was put in the bundle for winter, and then the bundle was reclosed.

Fall was also an important time to honor Ninastakis, Chief Mountain. John Palliser of the British Boundary Commission Survey team noted that the Indians met in full view of Chief Mountain and performed some "characteristic dances." These surveyors might have observed a ceremony associated with bundle openings.[49] Traditionally, women joined in round dances around the drum and did the owl dance and a partner dance; the men did the grass dance, a distinctly Blackfeet dance. Any of these may have been what Palliser witnessed at the foot of Chief Mountain back in 1859.

Chief Mountain T. J. Hileman, photographer, Glacier National Park, 3173

Blackfeet woman making parfleches, 1908 Walter McClintock, photographer, Yale Collection of Western Americana, Beinecke Rare Book and Manuscript Library, Yale University, New Haven, Connecticut, 1090225

In general, fall was the time when the people began to prepare for winter. They hunted, and they prepared dry meat and *mokimaani*, a mixture of dry meat and berries. Places like the Cutbank Creek headwaters were especially good for hunting at this time of year. Men hunted stray buffalo bulls, taken for their hides to make parfleches. The women would also use the hides to tie their travois with. The hair on the buffalo's head was made into ropes. And the women made a string from the sinews to be used when they tanned the skins for their lodges.[50]

Early fall was an important time of year to be able to assess the signs in nature regarding the type of winter that would be experienced. In addition to the celestial signs described earlier, our ancestors watched plants and animals for other signs. Blue grama grass was used to predict the winter. "If the culm had but one fruit spike, the winter would be mild. If it had two or more, the winter would be correspondingly severe."[51]

Animals know about the winter ahead, and they build their homes accordingly. By watching them, the people also knew what to expect. Caroline Russell learned from her Kainai grandmother that ants will build a tall structure if it's going to be a big snow winter with a wet spring. If the season will be dry, their home will be low to the ground, where the wind can't dry it out. Where muskrats build their dens will tell about the coming winter. If the den is close to the bank, the winter will be mild; if it is out in the lake, where the water is deep, it will be a cold winter, and the den will protect them from becoming frozen in and trapped in their dens. Beavers, too, build dams very deep in the water when the winter will be long and cold. Watching the sky is another way to predict the weather. If you see geese flying high and fast, prepare for a very cold season ahead.[52]

Animal organs and entrails of birds can also be read to inform people about the winter. Edmond "Wishy" Augare explained that the proportion of length to width of a deer or elk spleen will tell about the winter weather to come. This knowledge has been passed down through the generations.[53]

Saiaiksi Itomatoyii (October), or "When the Geese Leave"

Also known as "When Winter Starts," "First Big Storm," "When Leaves Fall Off," and "Turning White Moon" (for the animals that change color)

About the time when the geese fly south was the most important buffalo hunt of the year. The people watched for the signs that would tell them when to hunt for the best meat. The Blackfeet recognized that buffalo cows were prime and in the best condition for hunting in the fall when the spear grass was spread out. (At maturity, the previously erect seed-bearing culms flatten onto the soil surface.)[54]

Even though people generally could count on fresh meat all winter, they readied themselves for the possibility of going without by preparing great stores of dried meat and pemmican. The important work of hunting chiefs was described by Calf Tail and recorded by Donald Collier in 1934:

> The band chief announces the need for meat and tells the people to go out to hunt, and announces who will be the leader of the hunting party. This all has been decided in a smoke meeting of the prominent men. The chief remains in camp. Of the hunting party the members follow the orders of the leader. If any disagree with him they are free to leave the party and hunt by themselves. When the herd is located, the leader directs the approach of the hunters and no charge is made until he gives the word.

Calf Tail remembered that at the beginning of the winter of 1873–1874, each of his father's four wives had four parfleches of dried buffalo meat, each weighing fifty to sixty pounds. Eight parfleches was considered a good store of dried meat for a family.[55]

The fall was also a time to go to the hills and mountains for harvesting lodge poles along with "sweet pine" for use as a smudge. Sweet pine is actually alpine fir. While men were busy with their activities, the women processed meat and berries and made pemmican for the winter. Robes were also prepared for trade. The roots of wild rhubarb were gathered, then split and cut up and dried for winter use. Sometimes these roots were dipped in animal blood before being dried. When prepared for meals, the dried roots were boiled and sweetened.

The Blackfeet were known for their ingenious methods of capturing large numbers of buffalo at one time. They were famous for their *pis'kuns*, or "deep kettles of blood," the result of driving buffalo into a predetermined enclosure. One important activity at this time of year was for men to go out and repair and strengthen the pis'kuns, so they would be in good order for winter. They would set snares for wolves in the corral, arranged so as to jerk the wolf in the air. The wolf skins were then used as robes by the men when they ran the buffalo toward the pis'kun.

Pis'kun Walter McClintock, photographer, Yale Collection of Western Americana, Beinecke Rare Book and Manuscript Library, Yale University, New Haven, Connecticut, 1089808

As recorded by George Bird Grinnell, the pis'kun

> was an enclosure, built out from the foot of a perpendicular cliff
> or bluff, and formed of natural banks, rocks and log or brush—
> anything in fact to make a close, high barrier. In some places
> the enclosure might be only a fence of bush but even here the
> buffalo did not break it down, for they did not push against it, but
> ran round and round within, looking for a clear space through
> which they might pass. From the top of the bluff, directly over
> the pis'kun, two long lines of rock piles and brush extended far
> out on the prairie, ever diverging from each other like the arms of
> the letter V, the opening over the pis'kun being at the angle. . . .
> In winter, when the snow was on the ground, and the buffalo
> were to be led to the pis'kun, the following method was adopted
> to keep the herd travelling in the desired direction after they had
> got between the wings of the chute. A line of buffalo chips, each
> one supported on three small sticks, so that it stood a few inches
> above the snow, was carried from the mouth of the pis'kun straight
> out toward the prairie. . . . This line was, of course, conspicuous
> against the white snow, and when the buffalo were running down
> the chute, they always followed it, never turning to the right nor
> to the left.[56]

This was a technique taught to the people by Napi in the beginning, but it
was used less often once horses became an important part of the culture.

Winter camp locations were scouted out in October or November. The
head chief would consider the information from the scouts and then, with
the advice of the band chiefs, select a location that would fit the needs
of the tribe. The ideal locations were among stands of trees in protected
valleys, where people were sheltered from the snow and cold winter winds.

Trapping of fur-bearing animals began around the middle of October, when the hides were good and thick. This month was known by the
Blackfeet as "Turning White Moon" because it is the month the weasel
and the plains rabbit, their fur having had a brownish tint in the summer
in order to provide a form of camouflage, turns pure white.[57]

Rabbits, hunted by youngsters, were obtained for food and clothing.
Jim White Calf explained to Claude Schaeffer how young people would
"surround a thicket and dispatch them with whatever weapon they had,
bow & arrows, spears, clubs or even rocks." He told of how the women
would cut the rabbit hides into strips, which were then twisted and joined
together, like a rag rug. Another use of the rabbit skin was as the material

for a short jacket. Some strict rules applied for bundle holders regarding exposure to rabbit fur.[58]

Although antelope meat was not relished—because of its sagey flavor and stringy texture—the thin, lightweight hides were valued for many light utility needs. From antelope hides, women would make children's summer clothes and also use these hides to wrap some of the birds in the bundles.

Once the white traders were established in Blackfeet country, the men hunted for wolves, badgers, skunks, antelopes, and buffalo at this time of year so they would have hides and pelts to trade. The trading fort was part of their seasonal round, and they all looked forward to the goods that would be acquired through trade.

Iitommohkohpoota (November), or "When the Big Snow Comes"

Also known as "When Winter Starts," "When Geese Fly South," "When Big Winds Blow," and "Moon to Knock Bullberries Off Their Thorny Bushes"

As winter drew near, and the buffalo again moved up close to the mountains, the announcement would go out that it was time to move to winter camps. Once there, women and children got to work immediately gathering wood for the winter while men prepared for hunting. According to our elders,

> The women would go on foot for wood. They would pack the wood on their back. When the wood was far to get, they would put the travois on a horse. They had covered their saddles from one end to the other [with rawhide]. They carried wood on them [on the travois and the saddles]. . . . When they had done carrying wood . . . , then they began to coil up the ropes attached to the travois [for fear] that [the ropes] . . . might be eaten [by the dogs].[59]

With the coming of winter came a time of intensive teaching, when old ones recounted the happenings of the day and of the past. When the first snow came is when they told the Napi stories, the mythical stories of how we came to be.

During the early winter, buffalo were prime and fat. Full tribal participation was needed to conduct successful hunts in order to acquire the winter supply of buffalo meat. When buffalo were spotted nearby, the chief

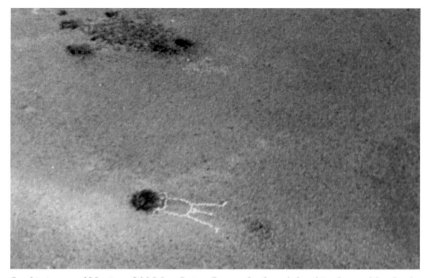

In this image of Napi on Old Man Lying Butte, the figure's head is obscured by shrubs.
Schultz Collection, Merrill G. Burlingame Special Collections, Montana State University Libraries, Bozeman, 525

would announce that in the morning the men should be ready to hunt. Sometimes when buffalo were sighted and conditions were just right, the men would get in place along the drive lines to a pis'kun while others, on horseback, would initiate the buffalo drive. The last known buffalo drive using a pis'kun was on the Teton River, close to the mountains, in the 1870s. This pis'kun is located just a few miles from the place where Napi lay down to rest and left an image of himself on Old Man Lying Butte.

When the men returned from the hunt, the women had work to do preparing more food for the winter. Once a woman had finished gathering her wood, she would begin the task of turning the buffalo's leg bones into soup:

> She pulled out her stone to hammer the bones on, [and] her stone-hammer. She put the leg-bones down on her half of a hide. She would say: I shall make grease [from the bones]. Then she began to hammer them. She had already put her . . . pot on the fire. She would make the soup with one of the leg-bones. . . . Then she would put the mashed bones in [the pot]. When it had boiled a long time, then she would pull it from the fire. She had already put the cherries [near her]. She took a horn-spoon. With that she skimmed. She put her skimmed grease in a big . . . bowl. When she had done skimming [the grease], she put the cherries in [the bowl]. . . . She told the women: You must get hot this soup of

the leg-bones. Her daughter was already hammering the sirloin-dried-meat. [When] she had done hammering, she gave it to [her mother]. And [the mother] mixed it up with the skimmed grease [and cherries]. Then she made it all into one roll. She gave that to her son-in-law. He invited the old men.[60]

Another important job after the hunt was tanning the hides. The women would be in a hurry for their robes, wanting to make sure that their families stayed warm when the cold weather hit. To ready the hides, the women jerked the meat from the skin of the hides, scraped them, oiled them with the brains and the liver, and then greased them. With water heated in a pot on the fire, they would soak them through so they could be stretched. By twisting the hides, they would remove the excess water. Then they pegged them down, fully stretched, and began to scrape the moisture out of them with a stone scraper. They would brush the hair side with sticks. Then they stretched the hide by stepping on it, by holding their feet on the ends. They used buffalo shoulder blades to finish off the hide. With the job done, they had little more to worry about since they had robes for themselves, their husbands, and their children. They would all sleep in comfort.[61]

Woman tanning a hide, 1904 Walter McClintock, photographer, Yale Collection of Western Americana, Beinecke Rare Book and Manuscript Library, Yale University, New Haven, Connecticut, 1089832

The men hunted other animals as well as buffalo. Elk and deer were hunted as were sheep and goats. Bighorn sheep hides gathered at this time of year were turned into headdresses for use in ceremonies.

In late November 1885, James Willard Schultz encountered a group of North Piegans camped at the exit of Upper St. Mary Lake, successfully hunting goat and sheep.[62] This was a few years after the last buffalo hunt, when the people had to focus on other kinds of meat to survive. Even though the U.S. government had promised food in exchange for land, the people starved if the winter was rough and meat couldn't be acquired.

Snowshoes were an important adaptation to life at the edge of the Rockies. In 1949, Yellow Kidney told Claude Schaeffer about the origins, uses, and construction of the various types of snowshoes. He told of the people being shown "by a boy from the west side of the mountains how to use them." In the old days, they made the snowshoes before a storm "so as to be ready." The snowshoes had laces of rawhide and were slightly turned up in front with a "tail at the back." They were used mainly "in the period before horses" and were used when hunting buffalo, elk, deer, and antelope in deep snow, where the animals floundered. Yellow Kidney told Schaeffer that snowshoes were used only by hunters—though sometimes by young runners in going to another camp for native tobacco—and never by women and children. They were highly prized and cared for. Yellow Kidney added that snowshoes were made of serviceberry wood in a two-piece construction.

> [They were m]ade in various lengths—about the height of a seated man. Rawhide for the netting was taken from the thick hide of a buffalo's shoulder, to resist moisture better. . . . A twisted thong was run across the snowshoe as the solitary crosspiece. . . . There was a loop across for [the] toe hold. . . . They were used with double moccasins, an inner one of buffalo hide with the hair inside, and an outer one of elk hide.

He said snowshoe users employed two poles made of green cherry wood. They were cut and bent at the upper ends to form a shepherd's crook, then wrapped with rawhide for a hand hold.[63]

Horses were challenged to get enough food when the snow accumulated. Walter McClintock was impressed by the instincts of Blackfeet horses after a fall snow, when he saw them pawing away the snow with their forefeet in order to expose the grass in an open meadow. When the snow was too deep for rustling, they were forced to forage for other sources of

Horse breaking through snow to reach the grass Walter McClintock, photographer, Yale Collection of Western Americana, Beinecke Rare Book and Manuscript Library, Yale University, New Haven, Connecticut, 1046292

sustenance. For instance, "one food substitute in winter for Indian ponies was the bark of the cottonwood tree, which is nourishing and palatable. If an Indian camp was near a growth of these trees and the people had no summer-cured hay, the women felled large trees from which they stripped the bark for food for their horses. Although the horses were hardy, their winter lot was at the best a hard one, and they were apt to come out of it in the spring in a reduced and weak condition." McClintock noted that a "city-bred" horse would have starved under these conditions.[64]

Otsstoyiiwa (December), or "When the Cold Comes"

Also known as "When the Buffalo Calves Are Black"

Winter is the time of storytelling and all-night ceremonies. The people have always understood winter as the time for sleep and regeneration, when that spirit from the north blows onto the Mother Earth its power, the snow. All of the beauty of the Mother Earth is covered over by the snow-white blanket of the northern spirit. Underneath this blanket all life goes to sleep as though dead.

Winter camps were arranged along rivers for fresh water and where firewood could easily be found to keep the lodges warm. Cutbanks,

Winter camp with Heavens Peak in background Walter McClintock, photographer, Yale Collection of
Western Americana, Beinecke Rare Book and Manuscript Library, Yale University, New Haven, Connecticut, 1090099

massive old cottonwoods, and thickets of poplars and willows in these
valley settings provided fuel as well as protection from cold winds. One
favorite wintering site was at St. Mary, or "Lakes Within," by the place
where the Beaver Bundle originated. All winter long the Beaver Bundle
holders would notch into their calendar sticks the passing of each day,
keeping track of the right time for their spring Beaver ceremonies.

On cold, windy nights the children would sit around the warm tipi
lodges and listen to the elders recount the beautiful myths, legends,
history, and adventures of their tribe. Napi stories could only be told
during the season when snow was on the ground and there were no leaves
on the trees. In addition to these ancient teachings, the elders would tell
the children about their brave Blackfeet warriors who had counted many
coups. Other stories of exciting hunting trips would help pass the long
winter months.

During storms and long cold spells, the people were snug in their
lodges, sitting around the fire talking about daily life while they mended
things, and telling legends and tales of adventures into the night. They
might play stick games until the storm subsided. The women amused
themselves by gambling with four bones, which they threw upon the

ground and called by name. Men used four hiding-sticks of bone, one marked with a black ring. They formed two sides, each with a leader who was an expert in handling the bones. The side with the bones drummed with sticks on the lodge poles; they sang songs while they played and made jibes, trying to rattle the guessers. In this way, the play went on until one side had lost all the counting-sticks. In this game, the players wagered weapons, horses, saddles, sometimes their tipis, and sometimes everything they possessed.[65]

With buffalo seeking the same protection as the people in the valley bottoms, buffalo hunting continued into this moon "when the buffalo calves are black." As Dick Sanderville told Donald Collier in 1938: "Except in bad weather, it was always possible to get fresh meat, buffalo, deer, antelope. If [the people] were well prepared with dried stores and generally successful in bringing in fresh meat, they would have some dried meat left in the spring."[66]

When people had to go out, they traveled with care, knowing how easily Cold-maker could destroy them. Grinnell observed that wolf skins were used as lining for yearling and two-year-old buffalo skins to keep people warm. Otter fur, turned inside out, was used for gloves, socks, and caps to keep people warm and dry. Alex Johnston learned that "when on horse-stealing expeditions in winter, the Indians protected their feet by filling their moccasins with dried bunch grass." He concluded that the material was probably sedge, since the softer dried leaves of sedge are useful for this purpose.[67]

Kaatoyii (January), or "Snow Blind"

Also known as "When the Heavy Snows Fall" and "Helping to Eat" (because the cold weather would keep people from hunting, so they were forced to share remaining food supplies). A more recent name is "Kissing Holy Day Moon" for the dancing and kissing tradition on New Year's Day.

When the heavy snows of January prevented the people from hunting, they were grateful for their stores of dried meat, pemmican, and berries preserved during the previous months. There was little to do during these times except to play games and listen to the old people tell the stories that had been repeated around campfires since time immemorial.

After the buffalo had been exterminated, sheep, elk, and deer hunting became more important in winter. Based on observations by Grinnell and others, sheep hunting was good at Mount Altyn in the Many Glacier area, around East Flattop Mountain, and along Boulder Creek.

Winter plant foods consisted primarily of dried cakes and berries. Silverberry or buffaloberry, although not favored because of their sourness, provided emergency food for winter. These berries stay on their bushes and are reported to get sweeter during the winter. Even the inner layer of bark can be eaten. Buffaloberry bark is very tough and served as an alternative to rawhide for making strong rope. Oregon grapes and kinnikinnick berries were not favorites because of their strongly acidic taste, but they both could be consumed when needed.[68]

Winter camps were large, and much socializing occurred. The winter was a time for children up to sixteen years of age to play and compete against each other in traditional winter sport games, including coasting, top-spinning, sliding on ice, and other children's games. Boys spun wooden tops in the soft snow, driving them over the surface with whips of buckskin or bark. They also played a game on the ice using smooth stones like tops; playing in pairs, they spun the stones by whipping and driving them together. The top that spun the longest was the winner. They also used pebble tops on hard snow, making them jump while spinning across the holes by striking them with their whips.[69]

The most popular of winter sports was coasting down steep, snow-packed hills onto the valley bottoms. The sleds used for coasting were

Playing a game on ice Nicholas Point, *Wilderness Kingdom, Indian Life in the Rocky Mountains: 1840–1847: The Journals and Paintings of Nicolas Point*, trans. Joseph P. Donnelly (New York, 1967), 65

made entirely of parts of the buffalo carcass, without a single nail or bolt. The runners were five to ten buffalo rib bones—the long, heavy ribs of a buffalo cow, scraped free of meat and gristle. These ribs were separated from the backbone and breastbone and reassembled in exactly the same order as on the buffalo. The ribs were tied together at each end by a rawhide rope that wound in and around a crosspiece of split willow. The seat was made of skin from the leg of the buffalo, stretched hair side up over the runners and tied to the willow crossbars at each end. A buffalo tail was sewn or tied to the rear of the seat for decoration. A rawhide rope tied to the front allowed the sled to be pulled uphill and guided sliding downhill.[70] If children didn't have a toboggan, they could use a piece of rawhide, holding the front up with their hands.

Saomitsikisom (February), or "Unreliable Moon"

Also known as "Eagle Moon," "Unpredictable Moon," "More Big Storms," "Big Chinook," and "Short Moon"

The same activities were carried out all winter long, with storytelling and games continuing as the children began to be restless. Game was scarce near the camp by the end of winter and so people relied more and more on stored foods. While the men continued to hunt whatever large game was in the area—buffalo, deer, elk, and, if necessary, bighorn sheep—young people would continue to track cottontail rabbits through the end of winter. In the leanest of times, people would turn to the berries of wolf willow and other famine food.

Depending on the weather and meat supplies, the chief might call for a buffalo hunt:

> [When] the buffalo were far, when it was really warm weather, the chief would cry out over the camp: We shall go on a hunt. We shall go with pack-horses, and stay for some days. They took the small old lodges . . . [on the trip]. They went walking [slowly]. They would use thin willow-sticks for lodge-poles. [Where] men had two wives, their younger wives would go [with them] on a hunt. . . . Then they [the younger wives] were called "the chief-woman of the pack-hunt."[71]

Storytelling continued in the warm lodges. Some stories taught how to look into the future by observing the warnings of animals, how to know the different moons by watching the changes of the seasons and by studying the habits of birds and other animals, and how to know the signs in the heavens. If they heard the boom of a bursting tree followed by the boom of a water-filled hollow, they knew to expect more bad weather.[72]

Walter McClintock experienced the onset of a chinook one winter evening, when he was camped up against the mountain front:

> The south wind rose and the river was covered with mist. Misty clouds hung along the horizon, and I saw two rainbows at a distance from the sun. Banks of heavy clouds settled low over the Rocky Mountains, with another great bank higher up. In the west the sky became as black as ink and the color of indigo at the zenith. The wind went down and there came a strange stillness.
>
> Suddenly, from out of the west I heard a dull roar, like the roll of distant thunder. "Listen!" cried the scout. "The Chinook! At last! Good-Old-Man comes from the mountains to run out over the plains."
>
> I looked towards the Rockies and saw dense clouds of snow swept into the air by the force of a mighty wind. It passed the foothills and came swiftly over the plains, like banks of driven fog. Then the gale struck us carrying masses of melting snow, which covered us from head to foot. In a few minutes the temperature rose forty degrees.[73]

Men and women made sure that their tools and supplies were refurbished for the time ahead, when a more active life returned, and they hoped that their wood supply was sufficient. If people smelled *miss-is-a-misoi,* or "stink-wood" (wolf willow), burning, everyone knew some woman had been too lazy to gather enough wood. By the end of the season, only stink-wood remained anywhere near the camp, so lazy wood gatherers were forced to use this source of fuel and thereby be humiliated in front of the entire camp.

As the winter drew to a close, Beaver Men turned over the seventh stick and declared the end of the winter season. New symbols were added to the winter counts to remind the people of their shared history. The people gave thanks for surviving another year and looked forward to the rebirth of new life all around them.

Chapter 7

◈

Continuing Traditions in the Twenty-First Century

by Sally Thompson

After reading these accounts of the traditional seasonal rounds of the Kootenais and the Blackfeet, you, the reader, might wonder about their importance today, given so many changes since the days of the buffalo. For many of you, it may be difficult to imagine that the old ways that underlie these traditions continue to have value. If you're from a culture that gave up its traditions in order to blend into the melting pot of America, you may have no reference point for this lifeway. You may doubt that anything from the past could be so important. But deep cultural memories are essential to the identities of traditional Indian people.

Twentieth-Century Adaptations

The loss of land to Glacier National Park in 1910 was just one of the limitations to indigenous cultural practices that occurred in the early twentieth century. The Flathead Allotment Act of 1904 allocated 160 acres of land to each male head of family on the reservation and 80 acres to each single individual. The remaining acreage was then opened to homesteaders, which decreased the land base promised to the Salish and Kootenai tribes in the Hell Gate Treaty of 1855 by some 60 percent.

Kootenai Falls, part of the Kootenais' traditional territory Arthur M. Baum, photographer, Montana Historical Society Photograph Archives, Helena, PAc 2009-7 A3.103

The story was no different for the Blackfeet people. Between the time of the Lame Bull Treaty of 1855 and the Ceded Strip Agreement of 1895, the Blackfeet lost millions of acres through a number of executive orders and agreements. Then, the implementation of the Allotment Act in 1907 resulted in the additional loss of about 10 percent of the reservation to homesteaders in 1911.[1]

The same meadows that had held tipis since time immemorial were now places settled by homesteaders, who were drawn by the same amenities—water, flat land, food resources, and shelter—that had drawn the Indians. For the Natives, those public lands that remained "open and unclaimed," to quote the Hell Gate Treaty, then grew in importance. Kootenai men continued to trap in the North Fork, Blackfeet families continued to cut tipi poles and gather firewood on the east side of the park, and both tribes continued to hunt and pick roots and berries in the mountains adjacent to the park. To this day, the Blackfeet continue to use their age-old fasting sites.

Gigi Caye remembers hearing her grandmother, Adeline Mathias, daughter of the last Kootenai chief, talk of the days when white men became more and more common in the tribe's traditional lands of north-western Montana. "When they first moved in," Mathias would say,

> they were pretty nice to the Indians. They would let the Kootenais stay at their camps for long periods of time; they'd just let them pass through their property on traditional trails. They were nice to them and welcomed them, and would even give them their hides to tan. . . . It's not like that today even though we're still here and still go up to our aboriginal land. But we can't access our traditional campsites up there on private land. Things have changed a lot since those early days.[2]

Cathy Hamel, Adeline Mathias's niece, remembers when she and her cousin-sister, Margaret (Muggs) Friedlander, were teenagers in the 1940s, and their family would stay in West Fisher, near Libby, all summer long.[3] Besides their family's camp, there would be thirty or forty other camps in the area.

Margaret "Muggs" Friedlander and Cathy Hamel, Kootenai, 2014 Sally Thompson, photographer

We all survived up there picking huckleberries day in and day out.
Five to ten gallons a day, every day for thirty to sixty days. We were
selling huckleberries for fifty cents a gallon. Now, we go up there,
we can't find anything. People talk about the cougar sightings, elk
sightings, and bear sightings . . . and they wonder why. It's because
people stole everything from them up there in the mountains. Our
grandparents used to tell us to pick a little bit and you leave some
for the bear to eat.[4]

Muggs Friedlander also remembers that a few years later, during summertime, she and Cathy would visit their grandparents at the dump in
Kalispell, where they lived in little cardboard shacks. According to Muggs:

There must have been four or five families that lived there. They
lived off the junk food that was thrown out—the garbage in the
back of the stores in Kalispell. When the paper fell off the cans,
the merchants would throw them away. When our grandparents
would pick them up and open them up, if it was fruit, I'd be so
happy. If it was peas or beans, I'd be mad. We'd never know what
was going to be in the can. It was a surprise.[5]

Cathy Hamel remembers these trips to the dump as the only time
she got fruit. "We'd go up there visiting them and get oranges, grapefruit,
bananas. They found a can up at the dump, and Mom said they opened it
up and it was jam. They were so happy that we had to have a jump dance.
They started singing and dancing. It was a celebration."[6]

The location of the Kalispell dump had always been about fruit for the
Kootenais. Gigi Caye explained that their ancestors had picked chokecherries in that very area before it was developed. But food wasn't the
only necessity they were able to obtain from the dump. Cathy remembers
that the Kootenai women frequented the dump looking for the hides the
white hunters threw away. The women tanned the hides for clothing and
moccasins, as well as for cash. In fact, Cathy says, "That's what they made
their living on."[7]

During the early decades of the twentieth century, Indian people had
to adapt to a cash economy, whereas formerly resources had been shared
and bartered. These challenging times continued for decades.

Smokey Rides At The Door has thought about the challenges his
Blackfeet family and tribe went through in those same years, particularly the dilemmas that his parents faced during World War II. While
his father was serving in the South Pacific, his mother moved to Seattle

Smokey Rides At The Door, Blackfeet, 2011 Sally Thompson, photographer

to work in the factories. "In those four to five years that they were away from home," he muses, "traditions weren't important. Survival was what mattered." During that span of years, his people began to adopt the "white man's attitude" in order to be accepted. The economics of the white culture was emphasized, and spirituality became less important.[8]

Another challenge of these decades was the growing environmental degradation. Before the dominant society seemed to take notice, Indian people were keenly aware of environmental changes and losses. Some readers might remember the tear-streaked cheek of Iron Eyes Cody in the "Keep America Beautiful" campaign of 1970.

Muggs Friedlander remembers that even in the 1960s, the elders would tell her they didn't trust white people, that white people didn't care about this Mother Earth.

> One great-uncle of mine, when we were picking huckleberries looked up at the jet line, and said, "See that 'jeet'? All that's coming down. That's gas that's wasted. We're not going to have any more huckleberries."
>
> That was in 1962. I never believed it, but now we are losing everything. Everything is contaminated with all they build. They

say they're helping, but they're destroying our food and probably our health. . . . I used to hear Mom say, they're not helping us; they're ruining the land. A lot of it is caused by greed. They don't live with the way things are; they want to develop everything.⁹

Cultural Continuity and Resilience in the Twenty-First Century

Given so much loss, it makes sense to question what has survived and why? What sustains a culture surrounded by so many conflicting pressures?

Covenants with the Creator

A concept common to Native Americans is that of their "covenant with the Creator." This understanding of an ongoing agreement between a group of people and the Creator—that they have been given a homeland where they will be provided for and in turn they agree to care for all the life of that place—is fundamental. This covenant is the basis for the respectful interrelationships—the love of and respect for nature—for which Indian people are known. For the Kootenais, who choose "stewardship of the land and resources based on the sacred covenant with the Creator," the realm of Glacier National Park has always been a part of this covenant. Cathy Hamel understands this cultural continuity in relation to a commitment to the Kootenai homeland: "Why we are still here," she says,

> is because we have been kept isolated. . . . .You look at the placement of the Kootenai people. We [the Ksanka Band] were put here in Elmo, Dayton, and Big Arm. Our kin up in Canada start right up there at Invemere, then Windermere, and down to Creston, and on down to Bonner's Ferry; that's the Columbia River Basin. . . . The Nupikas, the Spirits, have kept us here. We are put here for a purpose and that is to guard our Columbia River Basin, our water. That is why we are still here and that is why the Nupikas are never going to let us go."

She reflects that they are probably not doing enough: "The old people used to get up each morning to greet the sun," she says. "They would sing their song, thanking the sun for all it brings, for the life it brings. Everything is dependent on the sun—the rain, the clouds, the water in the rivers, and all the plants and animals. Not enough people continue this important spiritual practice."¹⁰

Cathy Hamel, who described the Kootenais' "covenant with the Creator" as an obligation to care for and respect nature, points out where the tree's bark has been peeled to get to the edible inner layer. Sally Thompson, photographer

The Blackfeet remember their covenant as well, as they fight to protect Chief Mountain, the Sweet Grass Hills, and the Badger–Two Medicine area—the sacred places and waters of their homeland. As Smokey Rides At The Door explains, "Our promise to the Creator for giving us our land was to defend and protect our territory."[11]

These covenants to care for all life in the places they consider home are still in effect for people who have not left their homeland and have not lost their spiritual direction. Those connections are the essence of being indigenous. Whether the covenant came through the songs and dances taught to the Kootenais at the place now known as Apgar and repeated every year since or through the songs and ceremonies connected with the bundles that the Blackfeet open each year, these covenants provide a deep

Sweet Grass Hills Doug O'looney, photographer, Montana Historical Society, Helena

sense of belonging to this Mother Earth, to this cosmos, rarely experienced by those of us whose families crossed oceans to get here, leaving our homelands and covenants behind.

These age-old covenants continue to shape the relationships, beliefs, and activities of traditional people. Smokey Rides At The Door explains how Blackfeet traditions are closely related to the environment:

> If you look at the various seasons that we have, there are specific creation stories that address specific environmental cycles, concerns, elements; the berries, the grasses, the land, the weather, the fire, the cosmos. When a person asks "why" about something in our lives, we have to go back to our stories and they will tell us why. For example, why the savisberry is so important to our ceremony of the pipes. . . . [T]hat is the holiest berry that we use. Before we can even eat, we pray with that berry. We dig a small hole in the ground, place the berry in the hole, and say our prayer, signifying the cycle of life. We have to be able to go out there and harvest it for these ceremonies to continue.[12]

Gigi Caye talks about her relatives—Cathy Hamel and Muggs Friedlander—and their ongoing connection to the traditional cycles of activities:

If you look at these two ladies, they still go up to our aboriginal lands, even at their age. There's that connectedness. And that's where our ancestors come back in; forever since the beginning of time our ancestors were up there, all through this area [northwestern Montana], even to Yellowstone and all [the way to the southeast]. These two still feel that connectedness. . . . They still get around up there. Not quite like when they were teenagers. They may ride up there and maybe walk around a little bit, but they still go up there. We all do. This whole community still goes up there to our traditional places. Glacier Park is a little bit harder now, so we don't go up there that much, but we go to the traditional places we can, more and more.[13]

Darnell Rides At The Door still gathers the roots, berries, and herbs of the traditional seasonal round, and her husband, Smokey, hunts the same animals that have always fed their ancestors, but they have had to adapt to modern conditions. For example, when Darnell picks bullberries (commonly called silver buffaloberries) in the fall near Choteau, some sixty-five to seventy miles from where she lives on the reservation, she doesn't make that trek with a horse and wagon, or on a horse, like in the old days. She goes by car. She'll "take one day, and go down there to pick the berries. Technology and modern responsibilities have caused changes," she admits, but "the berries are still important to us."[14]

One way in which indigenous people differ from others is in their belief that everything has a Spirit, even the rocks and things that non-Native people consider to be inanimate. According to Vernon Finley, in his Kootenai worldview,

> Everything has a spirit, everything has a place in all of Creation, there's a purpose for it. There are no extra parts. For example, the idea that we could possibly take one of the resources that are here and use it up and it wouldn't have an effect on all the rest of it. That could never enter the consciousness of a traditional 'Aq̓smaknik. So that's the worldview that was formed over all of these generations of how to carry yourself in all of Creation.[15]

Margaret Friedlander learned from her grandfather, Chief Mathias, that what guides them is spiritual:

> We were taught to believe that everything on this Earth has . . . spiritual powers—animals, fish, flowers, roots, trees, everything. Some of the people on their vision quests got the power of something. The power is shown by a song. Whatever they visualize, whatever was given to them, they sing their song. That's how I was raised. That's what I was taught by my grandfather.
>
> You recognize it . . . [in] their spiritual doings [and] gatherings. That's when you recognize who has spiritual power that was given to them by the spirits. They can sing for a flower, a weed, they can sing for a limb. They don't talk about God. They don't know God. They don't know the Bible. They only know what they were shown by the spirits.

Just like in the beginning of time, when the spirits gave songs to the Kootenais, Margaret explains, "They still talk. Owls talk to us, and they know. The owl right here in Dayton in 1995 told me my brother was going to die. And he spoke in English. He was in the tree. He says, '*Upanee, Joe Mathias*.' That's my brother . . . , and I begged him. But it happened. Oh yes, animals talk, they still do."[16]

Animal heads adorn the walls of the meeting room of the Kootenai Culture Committee in Elmo. Margaret explains that "these are the guys around here who helped us survive. Even though some of them have no songs, they're powerful." "Even rabbit," adds Cathy Hamel. "Everything talks to us—animals, birds, and trees, they all talk. Everything talks to us, even the rock."[17]

One of those rocks dropped in front of Margaret Friedlander's grandson one day, seemingly from nowhere. Margaret instinctively knew its significance. "That's yours," she told her grandson. "And you'll find out later why it came to you." As Margaret went on to explain,

> That's his traveling rock, that's what we called them. Rocks that the spirits will give you—drop in your path. [My grandson] hasn't found out yet what it's for, but he will. There are some that the spirits give you and you don't know what it's for at the time, but you'll find out later. Maybe in a dream or maybe they'll tell you sometime when you're out walking at night. I learned all this from my grandfather.[18]

Indian people often walk along with their heads down, as you often see in old photographs, but they aren't ashamed, explains Cathy Hamel. They were "looking down for the rocks and making sure that their passage was good. That's the spiritual power of this world that was given to the Indians."[19]

As we try to bridge two views of the world, it may be helpful to circle back to the story told earlier by Vernon Finley in "The Place Where They Dance" (see page 62). In regard to the tribe's connection to the place now known as Apgar, he explained that so many generations of their ancestors "have turned into the earth that's there, and so we have a connection to this place and some of the blood that is going through my veins was there at that first winter camp and that connection is felt and lives in all of the Kootenai people."[20] The ancestors literally feed them through the nourishment of plants that then breathe for the people and the animals. Reciprocity. The circle of life; it's not just a concept.

Continuity of Belief and Practice

Where the beliefs persist, traditions continue. As Darnell Rides At The Door explains,

> There are lots of ceremonies that people still practice; the Thunder, the Beaver, and the Medicine Lodge, on a yearly basis. And everything centers around the Medicine Lodge for the whole year: The gathering of berries, the foods you eat, the trees, the plants, everything is seasonal, right down to the cosmos—the planets, the sun, the earth and the moon, the stars. The reason that the

Medicine Lodge is put up the way it is, is to be in alignment with the summer solstice. We firmly believe in those things, and we've practiced it that way since antiquity. The times change, and that's a given because the environment somewhat changes too, but our traditions are still intact. And we will continue to do our ceremonies as long as we're able to pass them on to future generations. It's very important that our traditions stay. The ceremonies save people's lives![21]

In July 2013, Darnell and Smokey Rides At The Door sponsored a Medicine Lodge, an Okan. They had vowed to do this when a grass fire threatened their home in 2011. The fire went around their house and spared all the homes along its twenty-six-mile path. Darnell and Smokey vowed to "sit holy" for their community, and, through their fasting, invoke the power of the Sun to take pity on them and bestow power to heal the sick, help the tribe, help the Earth.

The Okan, with everything set up in accordance with the sun at the summer solstice, has been a way of life since time immemorial. Today, the Blackfeet belief in the spirit world remains strong. This summer gathering on Badger Creek in 2013 invoked the same ceremonies: the four-day fast of the Holy People; the hundred willow sweat; the sharing of the dried buffalo tongues; the capture of the center pole for the Medicine Lodge; the preparation of offerings; the cutting of the painted buffalo hide in an

Darnell Rides At The Door and granddaughter Camee, 2011 Sally Thompson, photographer

Okan Camp, Badger Creek, 2013 Sally Thompson, photographer

unbroken, narrow, circular band to tie the Medicine Lodge together; the retelling of the Scarface story as it has been told again and again through the generations; the blessings for each one present; the raising of the center pole; and the completion of the Medicine Lodge where the Sun would bless the offerings until they rejoined the Earth.

One afternoon, on the third day of the Okan, a storm approached the encampment from the north. One of the men, culturally knowledgeable as well as a science teacher, pointed out that hail was forming the white center of the storm front. A highly regarded weather dancer, down from Canada, glanced up at the sky and noted the speed with which the storm was approaching. Fast. A woman ducked into her lodge and returned with tobacco, which she offered to the weather dancer. He proceeded to use the tobacco as his offering while he prayed for this storm to change its course. All present watched in awe as the storm system shifted suddenly

Darnell and Smokey Rides At The Door, Okan Camp,
2011 Mistee Rides At The Door, photographer

to the east. Strong winds still affected the camp, but hail and rain did not. The rainbow that followed seemed like a sign that Napi's world was alive and well.

Spiritual life for the Blackfeet is not something relegated to Sundays. It's a way of walking through the world each and every day. According to Smokey Rides At The Door, if you examine our traditions, you will find that spirituality is foremost.

> We don't call our spirituality a religion, we call it a way of life, because that's what it is—a way of life. When you take your contemporary teachings and mold it with your tradition, you'll find that out there are more ways of approaching a situation, whether it's positive or negative, than trying to simply get a direct answer. Each person, in their deliberations to get the answers to their questions, has to go through a series of motions, emotions, and when you go through that series, you feel complete. It's a different way of knowing than the one taught in school.

Smokey adds, "When you talk about speaking to spirits, . . . you call upon people who went before you [and] are on the other side because those are the ones who can give you that help. In contemporary society, you just don't know where that help will come from."[22]

Concern for the Future

Not everyone in the Kootenai or the Blackfeet communities practices the old traditions, and this worries the elders. What will happen if no one steps up to take on the responsibilities of passing on the unique Native languages, the songs, the ceremonies, and the beliefs that define their cultures?

Darnell Rides At The Door is aware of the small number of young people who are stepping up, and she wonders what will happen. "It's not going to be that easy for Gen-X and the next generation. They know a little, but there's a lot of competition for their attention and they're losing their specific identity as Blackfeet people, which includes their Blackfeet language." Traditional beliefs and protocols for how to behave in the world are the basis for specific cultural identity, and this identity is essential for knowing who you are. Darnell explains,

> You need to know who you are and know where you came from to know where you are going. For me, strictly speaking about myself, I didn't know that I was being molded into this traditional Pikunni path that I'm on. If thirty-five or forty years ago anyone had said, "you're going to be a keeper of the Thunder Medicine, or the Beaver Medicine, or you're going to do Medicine Lodges and you're going to 'sit holy,'" I would have laughed at them and said, "No, I'm not."
>
> The old lady, my grandma Mary Ground, bought me my first Hudson's Bay blanket, with the stripes on it. She said, "Here's a blanket for you. Don't open it yet, just take and put it away." "Oh, all right. What is it for?" "You'll find out later," she said. She did the same thing with Smokey. She bought him his first Hudson's Bay blanket. Little did we know that we would need them at a transfer about thirty-five years later. I'm not sure how she knew; it just sort of happened that way. We were being groomed without our specific knowledge. Slowly but surely those things came to pass because that's where the teachings were.
>
> Hopefully similar seeds have been planted in young people who will step forward to carry on these traditions in the future.[23]

Smokey shares his concern about how few Blackfeet hold to the old values. "For many," he notes, "the only time they participate in the old ceremonial life of the community is at their burial. They want to have this simple, traditional ceremony."[24]

Among the Kootenais, according to Cathy Hamel, the majority of the community continue to believe in their cultural knowledge and traditions, even if they don't practice.

> They've all been taught but some don't practice; but, when they're in trouble, who do you think they go to? They go to somebody who will help them. . . . Every one of the Kootenai people knows who to go to, where to go to. That's how we have survived. . . . From gathering roots, to hunting, to car mechanics, if we need wood, if we need this or that, we know who the experts are.[25]

Traditionalists from both tribes affirm the importance of continuing to live life in accordance with the teachings that have been passed down, through story and ceremony, since the beginning of time. The continuation serves them as individuals and community, and it serves all life on this Mother Earth.

Gigi Caye explains that it's "our spiritual beliefs that make us who we are and make us unique, and that's what has kept us here." Smokey Rides At the Door believes it is more important to have traditional knowledge first, before acquiring an education in Western society. "When somebody comes up and asks you about the most basic, essential things, like 'Why did Napi do this? Why did the Sun, Natoosi, do this? And why is there a North Star? Why are these ceremonies the way they are?' To have the knowledge of what those old people brought forth for thousands and thousands of years makes you who you are. This is our unique identity."[26]

Some people might question why these old traditions and beliefs matter. Smokey explains what he sees as essential lessons from the Blackfeet worldview to help in these difficult times:

> Togetherness is very important. . . . If we don't stick together, our whole planet will perish. If you look at this on an individual basis, it's the same thing. As an individual person, as an individual family, clan, or tribe, if we don't try to work together or get back to that extended family concept that we've lost over the years, we're going to die, just like the earth is going to die.
>
> I think Western civilization is beginning to realize that by taking and taking and taking, our diminishment of the earth is

drawing near. Our glaciers are drying up. The ice caps are melting because of the warming of the earth.

The same thing goes for family. If we don't continue to protect what was taught us in our traditions of how we react within the environment, and if we don't pass that on to our family members, that togetherness won't be there. We'll be individuals and we'll perish as individuals.

We can continue to learn from our traditions. Acting from them, we will see the regeneration of Mother Earth and the people that are living on it. That's why Indian people are so important. We haven't ventured very far from that understanding of our connection to Mother Earth.[27]

All the rules for living in balance are held in these teachings, and these teachings are very different from those held by the dominant society. Darnell adds that their teachings embrace love that is difficult to put into words.

It's like an unconditional love for The People, for our families, for the very ground you walk on, for the earth, animals, plants, and for the insects, everything that's living and moving; part of your world, animate and inanimate—you have this deep, unconditional love and respect for. Because everything makes something. It comes from a simple molecule or a cell to the end product, whether human or animal or plant. You learn that without those you wouldn't exist. . . . Native people have always known what the scientists are only now understanding.[28]

Final Reflections

If we take a step back from wherever we sit at this moment in time, we see the Blackfeet and the Kootenais at the edges of Glacier National Park and recognize that these tribes, having given up vast tracts of land surrounding and including the park, struggle to preserve and sustain their ways of life against great odds. Glacier Park holds particular cultural significance for both tribes because its wilderness values have been protected. Both Kootenai and Blackfeet cultural representatives express their gratitude for what is preserved by the park.

But Glacier National Park, like the tribal homelands surrounding it, is also a remnant. This once vast expanse of wild lands, occupied by abundant plant and animal species, many now extinct, is threatened by some of the same forces that challenge tribal traditions.

The tribes and the park hold something essential for all of us. Like indigenous people all over the world, the Blackfeet and Kootenai continue to honor the reciprocal relationship that formed the essence of their original covenants, and wherever they can, they continue to act on this responsibility.

Whether you read this during a visit to Glacier Park or while at home, wherever that might be, carry into your awareness the continuing presence of the Kootenais and the Blackfeet in their homelands. Recognize their remembered covenants with the Creator. This land and the waters that pour from it are still guarded by those given responsibility for its stewardship by the Creator. They have not forgotten that the animals, plants, and even the rocks, through their songs and ceremonies, took pity and helped the people survive.

We all have an opportunity in this twenty-first century, as we watch the glaciers melting and the limber pine and pikas losing habitat necessary for their survival, to join the Kootenais and the Blackfeet in their efforts to protect all our relations along the Backbone of the World. Somewhere in our DNA, we all remember our covenant with the Creator.

Appendix

◈

Current and Historic Place Names
in Glacier National Park

As Known Today	As Known to the Kootenai
Akokala Creek and Lake	Place of Red Willows
Apgar area	A Good Place to Dance
Arrow Lake	Small Camas Lake
Baby Glacier	Ice Where the Goats' Children Play
Bowman Creek	Big Strawberries
Carter Glacier and Mountain	Weasel Collar
Cerulean Mountain	Black Bear Hat
Citadel Peaks	Hand Mountain*
Debris Mountain	Sacred Rock
Dutch Creek	Big Belly Man*
Gardner Point Mountain	Chief Coming Back
Harrison Glacier	Coyote's Daughter or Old Man's Daughter

*Stories that accompany these names can be found in chapter 4.

Birch trees growing along lower McDonald Creek Glacier National Park, HPF 8158

As Known Today (cont.)	As Known to the Kootenai
Howe Lake	Lost Rider
Kintla Nana Akuqnuk	Little Gunny Sack
Kishenehn Creek	No Good or White Fir*
Lee Creek	Standing Lodge Pole of a Medicine Lodge
Logging Lake	Where There's a Big Beaver*
Loneman Mountain	Wolf Gun
McDonald Creek	Where a Person Is Brought Back to Where He Started
Mount Geduhn	Chased in the Woods
Parke Ridge	Green-Blue Ridge
Pocket Lake	Broad Body
Pumpelly Glacier	Daughter's Ice or No Bear Ice
Quartz Lakes, Lower and Upper	Where the Rhubarb Is Long and Head of Rhubarb
Red Eagle Glacier	Old Woman Ice
Red Medicine Bow Peak	Red Medicine*
Roger's Lake	Traders Lake
Singleshot Mountain	Old Man
Snyder Ridge	Ear Fastened to Skin
Sperry Glacier	Coyote's Son Ice or Blossom of Wild Rhubarb Ice*
Square Peak	Sitting Porcupine
Starvation Creek	Dead Man's Creek
St. Mary River	Where Rawhide Was Stretched Across the River to Pull Tipi Bundles Across
Swiftcurrent Lake	Jealous Woman Lake*
Upper Waterton Lake	The Long Lake

As Known Today	As Known to the Blackfeet
Ahern Glacier	Spotted Ice
Ahern Pass	Where the Warriors Go Up
Baring Creek	Weasel Eyes
Belly River	Belly River
Boulder Creek and Ridge	Breaks the Tail or Mule Deer
Chief Mountain	Chief Mountain
Citadel Mountain	The Needles
Cutbank Creek	Cutbank Creek
Elizabeth Lake	Otter Lake
Flattop Mountain	On Top Prairie
Goat Haunt	Where There Are a Lot of Goats
Hanging Gardens	Where the Bigfoot (Caribou) Was Killed
Hudson Bay Divide	Wide Forest
Kootenai Peak	The Mountain Where Someone Froze
Lee Creek	Rope Across or Rope Stretched
Marias Pass	The Backbone
Old North Trail	Old Trail Passing by the Mountains
Rising Wolf	Red Mountain, Holy Woman Rock
Singleshot Mountain	Old Man, once Napi's Point*
St. Mary Lakes	Lakes Inside
St. Mary River	Bull Pound River or River of Many Chiefs Gathering
Swiftcurrent Creek	Swiftcurrent Creek
Two Medicine River	Place of Two Medicine Lodges
Waterton Valley	Where We Fought the Kootenais
Wilbur Creek	Mink Creek

The Belly River and Mount Cleveland Schultz Collection, Merrill G. Burlingame Special Collections, Montana State University Libraries, Bozeman, 229

Passes in the Park

Akamina Pass (5,840 feet) was once called "Low Ravine." Although the pass itself is outside Glacier's boundaries, the trail cut through the northwest corner of the park following a less steep route along Akamina Creek to the pass and then descended Cameron Creek to Waterton Lake. Rarely used during the summer because of mud, the trail, sixty-six miles long, required ten days of winter travel on snowshoes or nine on horseback.

Brown Pass (6,600 feet), accessed from the west side up Bowman, or Kintla, Creek over Boulder Pass, was used primarily by the Kootenais. To the east is "Hands of the Mountains," where the Kootenais could travel on snowshoes between the "thumb" and "forefinger," but mounted they had to travel around the "hand."

Cutbank Pass (7,860 feet) and **Dawson Pass** (7,500 feet). Familiar to many Glacier hikers, Cutbank Pass was commonly used by the Pikunni and less so by the Kootenais except when they were returning from hunting buffalo on the east side of the mountains. Historically, nearby Dawson Pass might have been an easier west-to-east route. These two passes, along with Two Medicine Pass, connect the Cutbank and Two Medicine Basins with the Middle Fork of the Flathead by way of Nyack Creek.

Gunsight Pass (7,050 feet) connects the St. Mary Basin with the Middle Fork of the Flathead. Grinnell and Schultz found evidence of winter use of the pass. Traveling through the area in the summer of 1891, they saw

Brown Pass Trail Glacier National Park, HPF 1840

Gunsight Pass Glacier National Park, HPF 3281

ten-foot-tall tree stumps that had been cut by the Kootenais when the snow was that deep, presumably to clear the trail.

Kootenai Pass (5,700 feet) is located within Glacier, but contrary to its name, it is geographically south of South Kootenay Pass.[1] Called "Where the Kootenais Go Up" by the Blackfeet, this trail connected a section of the North Fork of the Flathead Basin with the Waterton Basin. The pass was an important route for the Kootenais as both a snowshoe and horse trail.

Logan Pass (6,654 feet) precluded horse travel. In the nineteenth century, this daunting pass was generally used for winter travel by the Kootenais. This route over the mountains was known to the Kootenais as "Pull the Packs Up," or, literally, "Where Packs Are Pulled Up on a Line," referencing the steep cliffs near the top. People would travel this route on snowshoes heading eastward and then would return home over a more accommodating trail.

The Blackfeet did not use Logan Pass as a thoroughfare, although they hunted in the St. Mary Valley below. Kootenai elders reported to Schaeffer that they used the pass to travel eastward only in winter because of the likelihood of encountering Pikunni in the valley below during the summer and fall. However, Red Crow told Schultz of a well-worn horse trail used by Kootenais that "ran to the head of the long valley and then down the west side of the range to a large lake that the Koo-te-nai Indians called Sacred Dancing Lake." Precontact archaeological evidence on top of the pass documents summertime use, but cultural attribution is not possible.[2]

Marias Pass (5,215 feet) connected the Flathead Valley with the Two Medicine country, just as U.S. Highway 2 does today. The route followed a circuitous but gentle trail, generally following up the South Fork of the Flathead River to a ford, now flooded by Hungry Horse Reservoir. The trail then led to a ford across the Middle Fork near the mouth of Dirty Face Creek and then up Bear Creek to Marias Pass, opening onto the prairies of the Two Medicine country.

Red Eagle Pass (6,640 feet) provided another travel option for both tribes between the St. Mary Basin and the Middle Fork of the Flathead. On their 1891 trip, Grinnell and Schultz located evidence of an old trail up Red Eagle Pass from the east side and found it easy to follow, except for having to occasionally detour around fallen trees. Schultz wrote that "My Kutenai friend . . . said it was another one of his tribe's across-the-mountains trails, but that it had not been used for a very long time."[3]

South Kootenay Pass (7,100 feet), also known as Boundary Pass, is actually located to the north of Glacier. It was used by the Kootenai for travel between the Waterton Lakes area and the Tobacco Plains. The Tobacco Plains Kootenai called this the "Buffalo (Cow) Trail." The Blackfeet, who used the pass for hunting in the mountains, called it "Bad Luck Fat" after a hunting party was trapped by a bad storm, making it difficult to pack out the fat, meat, and hides of many elk and moose carcasses. This route was favored because it was almost always open, with few windfalls and little snow. Archaeological evidence from the Blakiston Valley indicates that the buffalo trail was used for more than eight thousand years.[4]

Swiftcurrent Pass (7,175 feet) was a good route into the Many Glacier area from the west side of the mountains. Starting from the east side in 1891, George Bird Grinnell followed "a well worn Indian trail" up Swiftcurrent Creek. Camping at Apekunny Flats, he found evidence of Kainai hunting camps all over the area: "Once these mountains abounded in sheep and goats, and everywhere . . . may be seen the sites of old Indian camps, with rotting lodge poles, old fireplaces and piles of bone and hair, showing where game has been cut up and hides dressed."[5]

Notes

◈

Chapter 1: The Land That Is Glacier National Park

1. A more complete version of this story, as told by Ktunaxa elder Wilfred Jacobs, can be found at the Ktunaxa Nation Web site.
2. White, "Fire on the Land."

Chapter 2: The Tribes of the Glacier National Park Area

1. "Montana Indians." The spelling varies from Canada to the United States. You'll see "Kootenai" in the United States and "Kootenay" in Canada. Anthropologists tend to prefer "Kutenai."
2. McClintock, *Old North Trail*, 404.
3. Schaeffer Papers.
4. Reeves, *Mistakis: The Archaeology*, 325–70.
5. Ibid.
6. Malouf Papers.
7. Schwab, Matt, and Askan, "Glacier National Park." These nineteenth-century band names reflect the spellings used by Claude Schaeffer.
8. G. G. Kipp interview.
9. Spelling differences reflect Canadian and U.S. variations. In Canada "Blackfoot" refers to the nations of the Blackfoot Confederacy, whereas in the United States, "Blackfeet" is the common term. "Peigan" is the common spelling for the tribes of Alberta, while "Piegan" refers to the Blackfeet of Montana.
10. Schultz, *Why Gone Those Times?* 147–48.
11. G. G. Kipp interview.
12. Dempsey, *Amazing Death of Calf Shirt*, 59.
13. The information in this and the following paragraphs is from Schultz, *Blackfeet Tales*, 49–58.
14. G. G. Kipp interview.

15. Dempsey, *Amazing Death of Calf Shirt*, 59.
16. G. G. Kipp interview.

Chapter 3: The Coming of White Men

1. Wheeler, *The Trail of Lewis and Clark*, 311–13; Thompson, *David Thompson's Narrative*, 370.
2. Juneau, Linda, "Small Robe Band of Blackfeet," 39.
3. Bigart and Woodcock, eds., *In the Name*, 9–12.
4. Finley interview.
5. Salish-Pend d'Oreille Culture Committee, *The Swan Valley Massacre*.
6. U.S. Congress, *Treaty with the Blackfeet, 1855*.
7. Ewers, *Blackfeet*, 297–319.
8. For information on the 1895 agreement regarding the Ceded Strip on the west side of the Blackfeet Reservation, see Walter, *More Montana Campfire Tales*, 105–24; Vest, "Traditional Blackfeet Religion"; and Harper, "Conceiving Nature."

Chapter 4: Knowing the Land

1. Finley, personal communication.
2. See, for instance, Schultz, *Signposts of Adventure;* Schultz, *Red Crow's Brother;* Holtz and Bemis, *Glacier National Park;* Schaeffer Papers; and Holterman, *Place Names*.
3. Schultz, *Signposts of Adventure*, 6–7.
4. Ibid., 8.
5. Ibid., 204.
6. In the late twentieth century, historian Jack Holterman drew on Schultz's research and that of other writers and consulted with Kootenai and Blackfeet elders. His research confirmed the same Kootenai place names within the park reported by Schultz, primarily on the west side, and added a few new names to the list. For the Blackfeet, only twenty-five to thirty place names from Holterman's compilation appear to be original due in large part to the confusion caused by Schultz's work. See Holterman, *Place Names*.
7. Matt interview.
8. Schultz, *Signposts of Adventure;* Holterman, *Place Names*.
9. Finley, personal communication.
10. Schultz, *Signposts of Adventure*, 223.
11. Holterman, *Place Names*, 100.
12. Schaeffer Papers.
13. "Moodus Noises."
14. Holterman, *Place Names*, 71, 117; Gravelle, personal communication.
15. Names assembled by Holterman, *Place Names*.
16. Matt, personal communication.
17. Bullchild, *Sun Came Down*, 127–36.

A Blackfeet Okan camp at Pray Lake Glacier National Park, HPF 1749

18. "Drawn by the Feathers" sketch map.
19. Moulton, *Journals,* 401.
20. McClintock, *Old North Trail,* 440.
21. Darris Flanagan, in his book *Indian Trails of the Northern Rockies,* provides
    an excellent compilation of major passes used by the Kootenai to cross
    the Continental Divide between lands now in Jasper, Banff, and Waterton
    National Parks in Canada and, to the south, through Glacier National Park
    and the Bob Marshall Wilderness in Montana and farther south. Flanagan
    thoroughly reviewed the work of early explorers and later researchers. He
    drew liberally on Claude Schaeffer's notes from interviews with many

Kootenai elders from the 1930s through the 1950s. Other trail information is available in Brian Reeves and Sandy Peacock's study of tribal uses of Glacier Park, *Our Mountains Are Our Pillows.* All of these resources contain detailed accounts of the Blackfeet routes of travel across the Continental Divide. This chapter draws on the same sources in describing the principal trails of the park area, adding details regarding minor trails.

22. Schaeffer Papers.
23. Flanagan, *Indian Trails of the Northern Rockies,* 30; Murray, "Marias Pass," 42.
24. Schultz, *Red Crow's Brother,* 182.
25. Doty, "Report," 105–16.
26. Grinnell, "Crown of the Continent," 670.
27. Schultz, "To Chief Mountain," 363; Reeves and Peacock, *Our Mountains Are Our Pillows,* 56.
28. Grinnell, "Crown of the Continent," 56.
29. Schaeffer Papers
30. Ibid.
31. Hamilton, "A Trader's Expedition," 79; Murray, "Marias Pass."
32. McClintock, *Old North Trail,* 51–54. Cutbank Canyon is culturally significant as the place where the buffalo were hidden by Crowfeather Arrow, as told by Percy Bullchild in this chapter.
33. Ibid.
34. Schaeffer Papers.
35. Flanagan, *Indian Trails of the Northern Rockies,* 30; Schultz, *Blackfeet Tales,* 44, 32.
36. Schaeffer Papers.

Chapter 5: The Kootenai Worldview

1. Schaeffer Papers. Ling are still present in the St. Mary and the Waterton Rivers of Glacier but are threatened by rising water temperatures.
2. Ibid.
3. Ibid.
4. Malouf Papers.
5. Schaeffer Papers.
6. Ibid.
7. Ibid.
8. Malouf Papers.
9. Schaeffer Papers.
10. Ibid.
11. Caribou used to be common in the old-growth forests west of the Continental Divide, near the International Boundary. With the demise of old-growth trees, the primary winter food source for caribou—lichen and moss—wasn't available in enough concentration to sustain the animals. A small caribou herd remains today in the Selkirk Mountains.

12. Williams interview.
13. Baker, *Forgotten Kutenai,* 31.
14. Ryan, personal communication.
15. Schaeffer Papers.
16. Hart, Turner, and Morgan, "Ethnobotany," 115–19.
17. Schaeffer Papers.
18. Hallock, "Marooning in High Altitudes," 402.
19. Ibid, 488.
20. Finley, personal communication.
21. Schaeffer Papers.
22. Ibid.
23. Ibid.
24. Ibid.
25. Greiser, "Artifact Collections."
26. Liz Gravelle, personal communication.
27. Schaeffer Papers.
28. Ibid.
29. Schultz, *Blackfeet Tales,* 153–54.
30. Ibid.
31. Malouf, "Economy and Land Use," 117–78. These sites remain good year-round hunting locations today.
32. Lefthand, personal communication.
33. Ryan, personal communication.
34. Hamilton, "A Trader's Expedition," 101. Hamilton noted that Kootenai women dug battle pits and that the guards made use of them on night duty.
35. Drying or boiling rids the fruit of its astringent taste and the toxic hydrocyanic acid.
36. Schaeffer Papers.
37. Grinnell, "Crown of the Continent."
38. Schaeffer Papers.
39. Nisbet, *Sources of the River,* 95.
40. Baker, *Forgotten Kutenai,* 33.
41. Schaeffer Papers.
42. Ibid.
43. Nisbet, *Sources of the River,* 106.
44. Schaeffer Papers.
45. Kootenai Culture Committee, *Ktunaxa Legends.*

Chapter 6: The Pikunni Worldview

1. Bastien, *Blackfoot Ways of Knowing,* 4.
2. Compiled from oral histories passed down from our elders.
3. McClintock, *Old Indian Trails,* 16.
4. Schultz, *Dreadful River Cave,* 24.
5. This story has long been told us by our elders.

6. Tatsey interview; Juneau, "Small Robe Band," 36.
7. McClintock, *Old North Trail*, 104–12.
8. Hungry Wolf, *Blackfoot Papers*, 2:393.
9. Curtis, *North American Indian*, 6:67.
10. Hungry Wolf, *Blackfoot Papers*, 2:401.
11. Ibid.
12. G. G. Kipp interview.
13. Matt interview
14. Bullchild, *Sun Came Down*, 76.
15. Darnell Rides At The Door interview.
16. Matt interview.
17. G. G. Kipp interview.
18. Schaeffer Papers.
19. Raczka, *Winter Count*, 25.
20. McClintock, *Old Indian Trails*, 49.
21. Ibid., 227.
22. Arlene Augare, personal communication; Cynthia Kipp, personal communication.
23. McClintock, *Old North Trail*, 486.
24. Uhlenbeck, *Original Blackfoot Texts*, 11.
25. McClintock, *Old Indian Trails*, 44.
26. Darnell Rides At The Door interview. Roots in general added important carbohydrates to a diet that was otherwise heavy in proteins. Carbohydrates are needed to metabolize protein. They are also rich in other nutrients.
27. Schaeffer Papers.
28. Reeves and Peacock, *Our Mountains Are Our Pillows*, 105.
29. Schaeffer Papers.
30. Bullchild, *Sun Came Down*, 94.
31. McClintock, *Old Indian Trails*, 156–57.
32. Ibid., 160.
33. Johnston, *Plants and the Blackfoot*, 15.
34. The Pikunnis refer to serviceberries as "savisberries," and that is the term used in this chapter.
35. Bullchild, *Sun Came Down*, 95.
36. McClintock, *Old North Trail*, 524–31.
37. Ibid., 44.
38. Grinnell, *Blackfoot Lodge Tales*, 207.
39. Schaeffer Papers.
40. Hungry Wolf, *Blackfoot Papers*, 1:130–31.
41. Ibid., 1:131.
42. Reeves, "Mistakis: The People."
43. Schaeffer Papers.
44. Ibid.
45. Ibid.
46. Hungry Wolf, *Blackfoot Papers*, 1:130.

47. Bullchild, *Sun Came Down,* 117.
48. McClintock, *Old Indian Trails,* 44–45.
49. Palliser, *Exploration,* 32.
50. Uhlenbeck, *A New Series of Blackfoot Texts,* 12.
51. Johnston, *Plants and the Blackfoot,* 19, 22.
52. Russell interview.
53. Edmond Augare, personal communication.
54. Hungry Wolf, *Blackfoot Papers,* 1:91.
55. Ibid.
56. Grinnell, *Blackfoot Lodge Tales,* 228–29.
57. Bullchild, *Sun Came Down,* 92.
58. Schaeffer Papers.
59. Uhlenbeck, *A New Series of Blackfoot Texts,* 11–12.
60. Ibid.
61. Ibid., 9.
62. Schultz, "To Chief Mountain," 362.
63. Schaeffer Papers.
64. McClintock, *Old North Trail,* 71.
65. McClintock, *Old Indian Trails,* 133.
66. Cited in Hungry Wolf, *Blackfoot Papers,* 1:91.
67. Grinnell, *Blackfoot Lodge Tales,* 261; Johnston, *Plants and the Blackfoot,* 22.
68. Hungry Wolf, *Blackfoot Papers,* 1:130–31.
69. McClintock, *Old Indian Trails,* 133.
70. Ewers, *The Blackfeet,* 148.
71. Uhlenbeck, *A New Series of Blackfoot Texts,* 13.
72. McClintock, *Old Indian Trails,* 149.
73. Ibid., 151–52.

Chapter 7: Continuing Traditions in the Twenty-First Century

1. The present-day Blackfeet Reservation consists of approximately 1.5 million acres and the Flathead Reservation approximately 1.3 million acres.
2. Caye, personal communication.
3. Kootenais, like many other Native American peoples, have no words for aunt, uncle, or cousin. These relatives are considered to be the equivalent of mother, father, sister, or brother.
4. Friedlander and Hamel interview.
5. Ibid.
6. Ibid.
7. Ibid.
8. Smokey Rides At The Door interview.
9. Friedlander and Hamel interview.
10. Ibid.
11. Smokey Rides At The Door interview.
12. Ibid.

13. Caye, personal communication.
14. Darnell Rides At The Door interview.
15. Finley, personal communication.
16. Friedlander and Hamel interview.
17. Ibid.
18. Ibid.
19. Ibid.
20. Finley, personal communication.
21. Darnell Rides At The Door interview.
22. Smokey Rides At The Door interview.
23. Darnell Rides At The Door interview.
24. Smokey Rides At The Door interview
25. Friedlander and Hamel interview.
26. Caye, personal communication; Smokey Rides At The Door interview.
27. Smokey Rides At The Door interview.
28. Darnell Rides At The Door interview.

Appendix: Current and Historic Place Names in Glacier National Park

1. "Kootenay" is the spelling used on the Canadian side of the border.
2. Schultz, *Signposts of Adventure*, 223; Reeves, "Mistakis: The People," 300–302.
3. Schultz, *Signposts of Adventure*, 108.
4. Reeves, *Prehistory of Pass Creek Valley*.
5. Grinnell, "Crown of the Continent," 669.

Bibliography

◈

Augare, Arlene. Personal communication with Sally Thompson, 2010.

Augare, Edmond. Personal communication with Sally Thompson, 2010.

Baker, Paul E. *The Forgotten Kutenai: A Study of the Kutenai Indians, Bonners Ferry, Idaho, Creston, British Columbia, Canada, and Other Areas in British Columbia Where the Kutenai Are Located.* Boise, Idaho: Mountain States Press, 1955.

Bastien, Betty. *Blackfoot Ways of Knowing: The Worldview of the Siksikaitsitapi.* Calgary: University of Calgary Press, 2004.

Bigart, Robert, and Clarence Woodcock, eds. *In the Name of the Salish and Kootenai Nation: The 1855 Hell Gate Treaty and the Origin of the Flathead Indian Reservation.* Pablo, Mont.: Salish Kootenai College Press, 1996.

Blackfoot Gallery Committee. *Nitsitapiisinni: The Story of the Blackfoot People.* Ontario: Key Porter Books, 2001.

Bradley, James H. "Affairs at Fort Benton, from 1831 to 1869." In vol. 3 of *Contributions to the Historical Society of Montana.* Helena, Mont.: State Publishing Co., 1900.

Bullchild, Percy. *The Sun Came Down.* San Francisco: Harper and Row, 1985.

Caye, Gigi. Personal communication with Sally Thompson, 2013.

Clark, Ella E. *Indian Legends from the Northern Rockies.* Norman: University of Oklahoma Press, 1966.

Conner, Roberta. Video interview by Sally Thompson, 2002. In possession of Sally Thompson.

Crowshoe, Reggie, and Sybille Manneschmidt. *Akak' Stiman: A Blackfoot Framework for Decision-Making and Mediation Processes,* 2nd ed. Calgary: University of Calgary Press, 2002.

Curtis, Edward S. *The North American Indian,* vols. 6 and 7. Cambridge, Mass.: University Press, 1911.

Dempsey, Hugh A. *The Amazing Death of Calf Shirt and Other Blackfoot Stories: Three Hundred Years of Blackfoot History.* Saskatoon, Sask.: Fifth House, 1994.

Diettert, Gerald A. *Grinnell's Glacier: George Bird Grinnell and Glacier National Park.* Missoula, Mont.: Mountain Press, 1992.

Doty, James. "Report of Mr. James Doty of a Survey from Fort Benton Near the Great Falls of the Missouri, Along the Eastern Base of the Rocky Mountains, to Latitude 49 50'N." In *Reports of Explorations and Survey, to Ascertain the Most Practicable and Economical Route for a Railroad from the Mississippi River to the Pacific Ocean,* H. Doc. 91, 33rd Cong., 2nd sess., 1855, serial 791, vol. 1, pt. 1, 543–53. Washington, D.C.: Government Printing Office, 1855.

"Drawn by the Feathers or ac ko mok ki a Black foot chief 7th Feby 1801" sketch map. Peter Fidler fonds. HBCA E.3/2 fos. 106d-107. Hudson's Bay Company Archives, Archives of Manitoba, Winnipeg.

Ewers, John C. *The Blackfeet: Raiders on the Northwest Plains.* 1958. Reprint, Norman: University of Oklahoma Press, 1983.

———. *Blackfeet Crafts.* 1945. Reprint, Stevens Point, Wis.: R. Schneider, 1986.

———. *The Horse in Blackfoot Indian Culture, with Comparative Material from Other Western Tribes.* 1955. Reprint, Washington, D.C.: Smithsonian Institution Press, 1980.

Finley, Vernon, Video interview by Sally Thompson, 2007. In possession of Sally Thompson.

———. Personal communication with Sally Thompson, 2009.

Flanagan, Darris. *Indian Trails of the Northern Rockies.* Stevensville, Mont.: Stoneydale, 2001.

Friedlander, Margaret, and Cathy Hamel. Audiotaped interview by Sally Thompson, 2013. In possession of the Kootenai Culture Committee.

Gravelle, Liz. Personal communication with Sally Thompson, 2010.

Greiser, Sally Thompson. "Artifact Collections from Ten Sites at Canyon Ferry Reservoir." *Archaeology in Montana* 27 (1986).

———, and T. Weber Greiser. "Blackfoot Culture, Religion, and Traditional Practices in the Badger-Two Medicine Area and Surrounding Mountains." Historical Research Associates, 1994. Confidential report prepared for the Lewis and Clark National Forest, Great Falls, Montana.

Gridley, Marion E. *Indian Legends of American Scenes.* Chicago: Donohue and Company, 1939.

Grinnell, George Bird. *Blackfoot Lodge Tales; The Story of a Prairie People.* 1892. Reprint, Lincoln: University of Nebraska Press, 1962.

———. "The Crown of the Continent." *The Century Magazine,* September 1901.

Hallock, Charles. "Marooning in High Altitudes." *Forest and Stream,* December 8, 1892.

Hamilton, William. "A Trader's Expedition among the Indians from Walla Walla to the Blackfeet Nation and Return in the Year 1858." In vol. 3 of *Contributions to the Historical Society of Montana.* Helena, Mont.: State Publishing Co., 1900.

Harper, Andrew. "Conceiving Nature: The Creation of Montana's Glacier National Park," *Montana The Magazine of Western History* 60 (Summer 2010): 3–24.

Hart, Jeff. *Montana Native Plants and Early Peoples.* 1976. Reprint, Helena: Montana Historical Society Press, 1999.

———, Nancy J. Turner, and Lawrence R. Morgan. "Ethnobotany of the Kootenai Indians of Western North America." Undated report to Ktunaxa-Kinbasket Tribal Council. On file at Ktunaxa Nation headquarters, Cranbrook, B.C.

Holterman, Jack. *Place Names of Glacier National Park,* 3rd ed. Helena, Mont.: Riverbend, 2006.

Holtz, Mathilde Edith, and Katharine Isabel Bemis. *Glacier National Park: Its Travels and Treasures.* New York: Doran, 1917.

Hungry Wolf, Adolph. *The Blackfoot Papers: Pikunni History and Culture.* 4 vols. Skookumchuck, B.C.: Good Medicine Cultural Foundation, 2006.

———. *Good Medicine in Glacier National Park: Inspirational Photos and Stories from the Days of the Blackfoot People.* Invermere, B.C.: Good Medicine Books, 1971.

Hungry Wolf, Beverly. *The Ways of My Grandmothers.* New York: William Morrow, 1980.

Johnston, A. *Plants and the Blackfoot.* Lethbridge, Alta.: Historical Society of Alberta, 1987.

Josselin de Jong, J. P. B. *Blackfoot Texts from the Southern Peigans, Blackfoot Reservation, Teton County, Montana, with the Help of Black-horse-rider.* Amsterdam: Johannes Müller, 1914.

Juneau, Linda. "Small Robe Band of Blackfeet: Ethnogenesis by Social and Religious Transformation." Master's thesis, University of Montana, 2007.

———. Video interview by Sally Thompson, 2008. In possession of Sally Thompson.

Kipp, Cynthia K. Personal communication with Sally Thompson, 2010.

Kipp, G. G. Video interview by Sally Thompson, 2009. In possession of Sally Thompson.

Kootenai Culture Committee. *How Marten Got His Spots and Other Kootenai Indian Stories.* Pablo, Mont.: Salish Kootenai College Press; Helena, Montana Historical Society Press, 2002.

———. *Ktunaxa Legends.* Pablo, Mont.: Salish Kootenai College Press, 1997.

Lefthand, Naida. Personal communication with Sally Thompson, 2010.

McClintock, Walter. *Old Indian Trails.* Boston: Houghton Mifflin, 1923.

———. *The Old North Trail; or Life, Legends and Religion of the Blackfeet Indians.* London: Macmillan, 1910.

McGillivray, Duncan. *The Journal of Duncan M'Gillivray of the North West Company at Fort George on the Saskatchewan 1794–5.* Edited by Arthur S. Morton. Toronto: Macmillan of Canada, 1929.

Mahseelah, Jon. Kootenai roundtable discussion, 2009. Videotape in possession of Sally Thompson.

Malouf, Carling. *Archaeological Reconnaissance, Vicinity of West Glacier, Glacier National Park, Montana, 1963.* Billings, Mont.: Montana State University, 1965.

———. "Economy and Land Use by the Indians of Western Montana" In *Interior Salish and Eastern Washington Indians.* Edited by Stuart A. Chalfant, Carling Malouf, and Merrill G. Burlingame. New York: Garland, 1974.

———. Papers. K. Ross Toole Archives and Special Collections, Maureen and Mike Mansfield Library, University of Montana, Missoula.

Mathias, Adeline. *How a Young Brave Survived.* Pablo, Mont.: Salish Kootenai College Press, 1986.

Matt, Pauline. Video interview by Sally Thompson, 2009. In possession of Sally Thompson.

———. Personal communication, 2015.

"Montana Indians: Their History and Location," 2009. Montana Office of Public Instruction Web site, opi.mt.gov/pdf/indianed/resources/MTIndiansHistoryLocation.pdf

"Moodus Noises," Discovering Lewis and Clark Web site, http://www.lewis-clark.org/article/1217.

Moulton, Gary E., ed. *The Journals of Lewis and Clark,* vol. 5. Norman: University of Oklahoma Press, 1983.

Murray, Genevieve. "Marias Pass: Its Part in the History and Development of the Northwest." In *Studies in Northwest History, State University of Montana,* no. 12 (1929).

Nisbet, Jack. *Sources of the River: Tracking David Thompson across Western North America.* Seattle: Sasquatch Books, 1994.

Palliser, John. *Exploration—British North America; Papers Relative to the Exploration by Captain Palliser. . . .* 1860. Reprint, New York: Greenwood Press, 1969.

Point, Nicholas. *Wilderness Kingdom, Indian Life in the Rocky Mountains: 1840–1847; The Journals and Paintings of Nicolas Point.* Translated by Joseph P. Donnelly. New York: Holt, Rinehart and Winston, 1967.

Provincial Archives of British Columbia. *Kootenay.* British Columbia Provincial Museum: Victoria, B.C., 1952.

Raczka, Paul M. *Winter Count: A History of the Blackfoot People.* Brocket, Alta.: Oldman River Cultural Centre, 1979.

Reeves, Brian O. K. *Glacier National Park Archaeological Inventory: 1993 Field Season Final Report.* Denver: National Park Service, 1995.

———. *Glacier National Park Archaeological Inventory and Assessment: 1995 Field Season Final Report.* Denver: National Park Service, 1997.

———. *Mistakis: The Archaeology of Waterton-Glacier International Peace Park.* Ed. Leslie B. Davis and Claire Bourges. N.p.: National Park Service, 2003.

———. "Mistakis: The People and Their Land, the Past Ten Thousand Years." Glacier National Park Archaeological Inventory and Assessment Program 1993–96. Final Draft Technical Report. 2000. On file National Park Service, Glacier National Park.

———. *The Prehistory of Pass Creek Valley, Waterton Lakes National Park.* Manuscript Report Series No. 61. Ottawa: National Historic Sites Service, 1972.

———, and Sandra Leslie Peacock. *Our Mountains Are Our Pillows: An Ethnographic Overview of Glacier National Park.* N.p.: Glacier National Park, 2001.

———, Mack W. Shortt, and Ken W. Karsmizki. *Glacier National Park Archaeological Inventory and Assessment: 1995 Field Season Final Report.* Denver: National Park Service, 1997.

Reiss, Winold. *Blackfeet Indians of Glacier National Park.* St. Paul, Minn.: Great Northern Railroad, 1940.

Rides At The Door, Darnell, comp. *Napi Stories.* Browning, Mont.: Blackfeet Heritage Program, 1979.

———. Interview by Sally Thompson, 2010.

Rides At The Door, Smokey. Audiotaped interview by Sally Thompson, 2013. In possession of Sally Thompson.

Russell, Carolyn. Video interview by Sally Thompson, 2007. In possession of Sally Thompson.

Ryan, Tim. Personal communication with Sally Thompson, 2009.

Salish-Pend d'Oreille Culture Committee. *The Swan Valley Massacre of 1908: A Brief History.* St. Ignatius, Mont.: Salish-Pend d'Oreille Culture Committee, 2008.

Schaeffer, Claude E. Papers, 1939–1969. Accession 2464. Glenbow Museum Archives, Calgary.

———. "The Subsistence Quest of the Kutenai: A Study of the Interaction of Culture and Environment." PhD dissertation, University of Pennsylvania, Philadelphia, 1940.

Schultz, James Willard. *Blackfeet and Buffalo: Memories of Life among the Indians.* Norman: University of Oklahoma Press, 1962.

———. *Blackfeet Tales of Glacier National Park.* 1916. Reprint, Ottawa, Ill.: Green Hill Press, *1992.*

———. *The Dreadful River Cave: Chief Black Elk's Story.* Boston: Houghton Mifflin, 1920.

———. *Red Crow's Brother; Hugh Monroe's Story of His Second Year on the Plains.* Boston: Houghton Mifflin, 1927.

———. *Running Eagle, the Warrior Girl.* Boston: Houghton Mifflin, 1919.

———. *Signposts of Adventure; Glacier National Park as the Indians Know It.* Boston: Houghton Mifflin, 1926.

———. "To Chief Mountain." *Forest and Stream,* December 3, 1885.

———. *Why Gone Those Times? Blackfoot Tales.* Norman: University of Oklahoma Press, 1974.

Schwab, Dave, Ira Matt, and Kevin Askan. "Glacier National Park North Fork Flathead River Culturally Scarred Tree Survey." 2005. On file National Park Service, Glacier National Park.

Smith, Allan H. *Kutenai Indian Subsistence and Settlement Patterns:*

Northwestern Montana. Technical Report. Seattle: U.S. Corps of Engineers, Seattle District, Washington, 1984.

Tatsey, Peter. Video interview by Sally Thompson, 2009. In possession of Sally Thompson.

Thompson, David. *David Thompson's Narrative of His Explorations in Western America, 1784–1812.* Edited by J. B. Tyrell. Toronto: Champlain Society, 1916.

Turney-High, Harry Holbert. *Ethnography of the Kutenai.* Menasha, Wis.: American Anthropological Association, 1941.

Uhlenbeck, C. C. *A New Series of Blackfoot Texts from Southern Peigans Blackfoot Reservation, Teton County, Montana.* Amsterdam: Johannes Müller, 1912.

———. *Original Blackfoot Texts from Southern Peigans Blackfoot Reservation, Teton County, Montana.* Amsterdam: Johannes Müller, 1911.

United States Congress, Treaty with the Blackfeet, 1855, 11 Stat., 657.

Vaught, L. O. "Glacier National Park." Manuscript on file Glacier National Park Research Library, West Glacier, MT.

Vest, Jay Hanford C. "Traditional Blackfeet Religion and the Sacred Badger-Two Medicine Wildlands." *Journal of Law and Religion* 6, no. 2 (1988): 455–89.

Walter, Dave. *More Montana Campfire Tales: Fifteen Historical Narratives.* Helena, Mont.: Farcountry, 2002.

Wheeler, Olin D. *The Trail of Lewis and Clark, 1804–1904. . . .* New York: Putnam's, 1904.

White, Germaine. "Fire on the Land: A Tribal Prospective." *Flathead Watershed Sourcebook* Web site. http://www.flatheadwatershed.org/docs/wpPDF/Popout_White_Fire.pdf.

White Calf Statement. "Proceedings of Councils of Commissioners Appointed to Negotiate with Blackfeet Indians." In *Agreement with the Indians of the Blackfeet Reservation,* 54th Cong., 1st sess., 1896, S. Doc. 118.

Williams, Leo. Video interview by Sally Thompson, 2009. In possession of Sally Thompson.

Wilson, Charles. "Report on the Indian Tribes Inhabiting the Country in the Vicinity of the Forty-Ninth Parallel of North Latitude." *Transactions of the Ethnological Society of London* 4 (1866): 273–332.

Wissler, Clark. *Ceremonial Bundles of the Blackfoot Indians.* New York: The Trustees, 1912.

———. *Material Culture of the Blackfoot Indians.* New York: The Trustees, 1910.

———. *Social Organization and Ritualistic Ceremonies of the Blackfoot Indians.* New York: The Trustees, 1912.

———. *The Sun Dance of the Blackfoot Indians.* New York: The Trustees, 1918.

———, and D. C. Duvall. *Mythology of the Blackfoot Indians.* New York: The Trustees, 1908.

Index

◈

Note: page numbers in italics indicate photos or illustrations

SALLY THOMPSON has spent over thirty years working with the native tribes of the West. Trained as an anthropologist (PhD, University of Colorado–Boulder), she has worked as an archaeologist, ethnographer, and ethnohistorian along the Rocky Mountains and in the Southwest. She has a particular interest in collaborating with tribes to implement unique cultural preservation strategies particular to each tribe or region.

As founder and director of the Regional Learning Project at the University of Montana from 2001 to 2010, she oversaw a team of specialists focusing on regional history, geography, and culture. During these years, she interviewed more than two hundred elders and educators from thirty-seven tribes and produced documentaries, websites, and DVDs with teacher guides. The Regional Learning Project creates opportunities for Indian people to speak for themselves about their histories and cultures. Sally lives in Missoula, Montana.

THE KOOTENAI CULTURE COMMITTEE, established in 1975, has as its mission protecting, preserving, perpetuating, and enhancing the language, culture, and traditional lifeways of the Kootenai people. The committee appointed Vernon Finley and Naida Lefthand to oversee the writing for this book project, drawing on oral history to re-create the traditional seasonal round. The Kootenai Culture Committee is based on the west shore of Flathead Lake, in Elmo, Montana.

THE PIKUNNI TRADITIONAL ASSOCIATION represents ceremonial leaders from the Blackfeet Reservation. Its purpose is to assist in keeping a positive and peaceful balance in the circle of life, emphasizing physical, mental, spiritual, and emotional well-being. Smokey and Darnell Rides At The Door took the lead for the group on this book project. These two South Piegan bundle holders worked with other elders to re-create their traditional seasonal round as it is dictated through their annual ceremonial cycle and through stories of history and culture. Smokey and Darnell are keepers of the Thunder Medicine (NaNampskaa) Bundle. Both hold the traditional rights to the Okan/Medicine Lodge ceremony with specific transferred rights to the Beaver Medicine ceremony, All Brave Dogs, and Painted Lodge Keepers. They are members of many ancient active societies of the Pikunni Confederacy.